The Story of My Life

First published in India in 2020 by HarperCollins *Children's Books*
This edition published in 2025 by HarperCollins *Children's Books*
An imprint of HarperCollins *Publishers*

Building no 10, Tower A, 4th floor, DLF Cyber City,
Phase II, Gurugram 122002, India

www.harpercollins.co.in

2 4 6 8 10 9 7 5 3 1

Text © 2020, 2025 Navajivan Trust
This book is published by the permission of Navajivan Trust,
Ahmedabad 380014 (India).

P-ISBN: 978-93-5357-637-0
E-ISBN: 978-93-5357-867-1

While every effort has been made to ensure the accuracy of the additional material presented at the end of the book, the publishers are not in any way liable for any errors that might have crept in.

All rights reserved. No part of this publication may be reproduced, stored in a retrieval system, or transmitted, in any form or by any means, electronic, mechanical, photocopying, recording or otherwise, without the prior permission of the publishers.

Typeset in 12pt/ 15.7 Adobe Garamond at
Manipal Digital Systems, Manipal

Printed and bound at
Thomson Press (India) Ltd

This book is produced from independently certified FSC® paper
to ensure responsible forest management.

The Story of My Life

Mohandas Karamchand Gandhi

Abridged and simplified by
Bharatan Kumarappa

Foreword by Tushar A. Gandhi

Contents

Foreword   vii

Introduction   xvii

Editor's Note   xix

Childhood and Youth	1
In England as a Student	29
In India as a Barrister	43
In South Africa	52
Visit to India	70
Back in South Africa	72
Back in India	86
In South Africa Again	90
In India and Founding of the Ashram	109
Champaran	113
Ahmedabad Labour	118
The Kheda Satyagraha	121
The Rowlatt Act and Entrance into Politics	126
The Birth of Khadi	131

Exploring Gandhi in Today's World   135

Foreword

Understanding Mohan

The autobiography of Mohan is a startling revelation. It is an intimate confession. Mohan is fearless in admitting his flaws and weaknesses. He opens his soul to the reader and illustrates the journey of a life from when he was little 'Monio' till people start calling him Mahatma. Mohan has told this story without any frills or fancy dressing. It is the story of a continuing voyage of discovery of the self. It is the story of Mohan's quest to discover his own soul and becoming able to listen to what he calls his 'still faint' inner voice.

Very few people have the courage to be so honest, especially public personalities who mostly prefer to keep their public and private persona separate. Mohan discards the difference between these identities and merges the two without any inhibitions to pen down his experiences, shortcomings and learnings.

What gives him the courage to be so brutally honest and bravely accept his faults and mistakes?

Mohan's transition begins in South Africa, where he emerges as an activist-crusader for the equal rights for Indians residing in this colony of the British Empire. It is here that he adopts the tenets of an ideal communal life by constantly experimenting with it. It is here that he takes the 11 pledges to live by in the ashram community he establishes in Phoenix near Durban in the Natal province.

Here he sets out on a lifelong quest to come as close to becoming an ideal human being as described in his favourite hymn, *bhajan* 'vaishnavajan toh tene re kahiye' – written by poet-saint Narsinh Mehta. For Mohan, it is a scale by which he can measure his evolution as a person.

The 11 vows of the ashram are ideals by which a dedicated and sustainable community can follow a moderate lifestyle. Before one reads Mohan's autobiography, one must understand what influenced him and what are the ideas that brought about the change within him that ultimately led to his transformation.

Ekadash Vrat, the 11 vows of Mohan: These are the 11 tenets by which Mohan lives and expects those who wish to join the ashrams established by him to live by. His ashrams are his experiments with establishing an ideal societal order – a sustainable way of life. The genius of Mohan is that these vows are timeless and have relevance even today.

1. **Ahimsa, non-violence:** Non-violence is a basic requirement to sustain life. There would be no life or civilization were it not for the age-old practise of non-

violence. The concept does not merely imply the absence of conflict. True non-violence means not to violate any living being's right to live and respecting their right to thrive.

Today, we are faced with a great challenge to our very own existence. Climate change is an irreversible consequence of our violence against nature. We are faced with a choice: non-violence or non-existence. From being a virtue, it has now become a necessity.

Not leaving behind a heavy carbon footprint, choosing not to avail more than necessary of nature's bounty, not being selfish, not harbouring prejudices, and understanding and respecting our differences. These are all examples of non-violence.

When food is kept in a pressure cooker, steam builds up inside it and creates pressure that cooks the food. But the cooker can only bear a certain amount of pressure. To avoid an accident, a weight is placed on top of the escape spout. When the pressure inside the cooker goes beyond its ability to withstand it, the weight is pushed open and the excess steam escapes, ensuring the safety of the one using it. The absence of a safety valve would lead to a catastrophic explosion.

Unlike the cooker, we do not have a safety valve. Tolerance is our best bet to have a safety valve, which can save us from angry outbursts. Those who believe in non-violence do not merely tolerate, they understand that every individual is different and so has a right to live differently. They understand and respect the differences.

Out of this, acceptance, respect and love are born. This is the ideal way of practising non-violence. This is the non-violence Mohan chose to adopt.

2. **Satya, truth:** Mohan adhered to the absolute Truth, he practised uncompromising truth that did not have versions. It was eternal and inviolate as the Sun and Moon. There is no deviation nor any convenient shortcut in this eternally existing truth. We have given different names to the embodiment of this truth. Some call it Ram and Krishna, some call it Allah and Mohammad, others Jesus, Guru, Buddha, et al – each as per their belief system. All these labels help us identify and give a name to the one eternal, invisible force, Truth.

   The quest of Mohan's life was the search for this elusive meaning, the quest for Truth. Education and knowledge are both pursuits of truth. Enlightenment is the realisation of truth.

3. **Asteya, non-stealing:** As a teenager, Mohan stole from his father but his upbringing and the values instilled in him troubled his conscience. Encouraged by his wife, Kasturba, he confessed his crime to his father and expressed sincere regret and asked to be punished. His father's tears were all the punishment Mohan needed. He repented and made a promise to himself never to succumb to such temptations and remained true to the promise till his last breath.

   Today, stealing has taken on so many meanings. It's not just material theft that is both immoral and illegal

but also the theft of ideas and creative works. Plagiarism, cheating in examination and fraud are all forms of theft.
It is also theft when we take more than our fair share of what nature provides and deprive others, the less fortunate ones, of their rightful share. Waste of food is also a theft from those who are condemned to perpetual starvation.
We often convince ourselves that it is a crime to steal only if one is caught. What we fail to realize is that stealing is a sin and a sin remains a sin whether one is caught or one gets away undetected. But the subconscious is always aware of one's actions; one can never cheat one's soul.

4. **Aparigraha, non-possession:** Today, we have become an exceedingly consumerist civilization, enslaved by our greed for possession. Our wants have outstripped our needs. We judge other's lives based on their possessions. Despite all that we possess there is one thing we never achieve and that is satisfaction. The irony is that even with meagre possessions, our ancestors lived a content life.
Mohan's life was a lesson in not only non-possession but renunciation. He gave up a thriving legal practice and voluntarily adopted poverty. As his life progressed, Mohan reduced his needs and lived a minimalistic life. He said, "Nature can provide enough for everyone's need but cannot provide for anyone's greed."

5. **Brahmacharya, celibacy:** Mohan observed chastity and fidelity. Brahmacharya in modern relationships also means honesty and being faithful.

6. **Sharirashrama, bread labour:** In the age of automation and artificial intelligence (AI), our physical activities are getting minimized. Mohan gives great importance to productive physical labour. He believes that everyone who consumes food must perform a certain amount of physical labour. Mohan reminds us that physical activities should be productive.

   Mohan shares with us that he spun a thousand yards of khadi yarn every day. The only time he did not do the spinning was when he was fasting. However, he continued to perform other physical activities. Most of us perform physical tasks only to keep fit. Exercising, cycling, running, swimming, sports, yoga etc., are some examples. Mohan reminds us how much our society is likely to gain if all of us were to take up some productive physical work. From a consumerist civilization, we would become a productive one.

7. **Aswad, control over palate**: Indulging in food is a sin for Mohan. His ideology of renunciation begins with controlling his palate, which means freedom from the enslavement of taste. Today, we have so many varieties of junk food that have zero or very low nutritional value. We would be healthier if we were to follow Mohan's advice and gain control over our palate.

8. **Sarvatra Bhayavarjana, fearlessness:** Mohan is terrified by all sorts of things. Fear holds him hostage. There is an anecdote about how during his childhood days in

Porbandar when there was no electricity, he was given the responsibility of lighting the lamps every evening for illumination. His elder brothers took this opportunity to have some fun at his expense. Whenever young Mohan entered a dark room, his siblings would extinguish the lamp and lock him inside the room. A terrified Mohan would beg to be freed and soon become hysterical with fright. The older children would enjoy Mohan's plight till Rambha, his nanny, would come to Mohan's rescue and calm him down. 'Rambha Ma', as Mohan called her, would console him by telling him that God was always there with him. So, there was no reason for him to believe he was alone.

Mohan refused to believe this. How could he feel God's presence beside him if he could not see God? Rambha Ma taught him to chant the name of Rama whenever he felt scared or threatened. It worked. Whenever Mohan tried this mantra, he was distracted from his fears and soon it gave him the strength to overcome his fears.

When you read Mohan's story in his own words, you will realize how fearlessly honest he is in writing about his mistakes and failures. The story of Mohan winning over his fears very much began with these incidents.

9. **Sarva Dharma Samanatva, equality of all religions:** According to Mohan, a true human is the one who makes it her/his duty to study all religious scriptures and respect every religion out of knowledge and understanding. Today, most religious prejudices are born out of

ignorance, false beliefs and half-truths, which lead to religious hatred and cause communal strife and violence. Mohan believes that the practice of religion is a private matter between a human being and what he believes to be God, and that it is a folly to believe that whom one believes to be God is superior to another one's belief.

10. **Swadeshi, use local:** During the pre-Independence era, England enslaved us by forcing us to consume goods from its factories and mills. They destroyed domestic crafts and traditional industry. Mohan realized this was wrong and launched a swadeshi movement – a return to the lifestyle of consuming local. The popularity of swadeshi ultimately made it unviable for the British to enslave us.

    In a world that is called a global village, sustainability can only be ensured if we adopt a local lifestyle. It is disheartening that we consume imported onions to keep the prices down while our local farmer is forced to dump his crop as he does not even get the minimum price for his produce. For every kilo of onion we buy which is produced abroad and exported, a local farmer here becomes more and more trapped in poverty and is driven to suicide.

    In several developed nations, the live local movement is being enthusiastically adopted. There is growing realisation that use of local produce is ethical and sustainable.

11. **Sparsha Bhavana, no to the practice of untouchability:** The practice of untouchability is a crime against humanity, a sin. How can some people be considered so inferior that even their shadow is considered capable of contaminating anyone it falls on? As a child, Mohan cannot understand why it is okay for him to touch and play with a calf but not with the child of a man who comes to clean the toilets in his house. On occasions when Mohan plays with the child or touches him accidentally he is severely reprimanded and is made to take a ritualistic cleansing bath before he is allowed to interact with others in the family or enter the home. Young Mohan feels this is unjust and wrong and vows to fight this evil tradition.

This is the story of Mohan, an ordinary human being, and his quest to make himself a better person. Mohan's story can become our story if we have the courage to follow in his footsteps. He started young, there is no reason for us to wait.

Tushar A. Gandhi
2019

Introduction

It is not my purpose to attempt a real autobiography or story of my life. I simply want to tell the story of my numerous experiments with truth, and as my life consists of nothing but those experiments, the story will take the shape of an autobiography. My experiments in the political field are now known. But I should certainly like to narrate my experiments in the spiritual field which are known only to myself, and from which I have derived such power as I possess for working in the political field. The experiments I am about to relate are spiritual, or rather moral; for the essence of religion is morality.

Only those matters of religion that can be understood as much by children as by older people, will be included in this story. If I can narrate them in a dispassionate and humble spirit many other experiments will obtain from them help in their onward march.

The Ashram, Sabarmati M.K. Gandhi
26th November, 1925

Editor's Note

Gandhiji's *Autobiography** and his *Satyagraha in South Africa*†, as published in English, run into almost 1000 pages. An abridgement‡ of these two into a single volume of 283 pages was published in 1952 by the Navajivan Trust. A request was received for a still smaller version for use in our schools. This book has been specially prepared to meet the need.

Matters which are not likely to be of much interest to school children have been omitted, and the language has been simplified where possible.

July 1955   Bharatan Kumarappa

* Published by Navajivan Publishing House, Ahmedabad-380 014, Popular Edn.
† Published by Navajivan Publishing House, Ahmedabad-380 014.
‡ i.e. Gandhiji's Autobiography [Abridged].

'I have nothing new to teach the world. Truth and non-violence are as old as hills.'

M.K. Gandhi

Childhood and Youth

Birth and Parentage

My father, Karamchand Gandhi, was Prime Minister in Porbandar. He was a lover of his clan, truthful, brave and generous, but short-tempered. He never had any ambition to accumulate riches and left us very little property. He had no education. At best, he might be said to have read up to the fifth Gujarati standard. Of history and geography he was innocent. But his rich experience of practical affairs stood him in good stead in the solution of the most intricate questions and in managing hundreds of men. Of religious training he had very little, but he had that kind of religious culture which frequent visits to temples and listening to religious discourses make available to many Hindus.

The outstanding impression my mother has left on my memory is that of saintliness. She was deeply religious. She would not think of taking her meals without her daily prayers. Going to Haveli—the Vaishnava temple—was one of her daily duties. As far as my memory can go back, I do not remember her having ever missed the *Chaturmas*. She would take the hardest vows and keep them whatever happened. Illness was no excuse for relaxing them. I can recall her once falling ill when she was observing the *Chandrayana* vow, but the illness was not allowed to come in the way of the observance. To keep two or three fasts one after another was nothing to her. Living on one meal a day during *Chaturmas* was a habit with her. Not content with that she fasted every other day during one *Chaturmas*. During another *Chaturmas* she vowed not to have food without seeing the sun. We children on those days would stand, staring at the sky, waiting to announce the appearance of the sun to our mother. Everyone knows that at the height of the rainy season the sun often does not show his face. And I remember days when, at his sudden appearance, we would rush and announce it to her. She would run out to see with her own eyes, but by that time the sun would be gone, thus depriving her of her meal. 'That does not matter,' she would say cheerfully, 'God did not want me to eat today.' And then she would return to her round of duties.

My mother had strong common sense. She was well informed about all matters of State.

Of these parents I was born at Porbandar, otherwise known as Sudamapuri, on the 2nd October 1869.

At School

I passed my childhood in Porbandar. I remember having been put to school. It was with some difficulty that I got through the multiplication tables. I recollect nothing more of those days than having learnt, in company with other boys, to call our teacher all kinds of names.

I must have been about seven when my father left Porbandar for Rajkot. There I was put into a primary school, and I can well remember those days. As at Porbandar, so here, there is hardly anything to note about my studies. From this school I went to the suburban school and thence to the high school, having already reached my twelfth year. I do not remember having ever told a lie, during this short period, either to my teachers or to my schoolmates. I used to be very shy and avoided all company. My books and my lessons were my sole companions. To be at school at the stroke of the hour and to run back home as soon as the school closed – that was my daily habit. I literally ran back, because I could not bear to talk to anybody. I was even afraid lest anyone should poke fun at me.

There is an incident which occurred at the examination during my first year at the high school and which is worth recording. Mr Giles, the Educational Inspector, had come on a visit of inspection. He had set us five words to write as a spelling exercise. One of the words was 'kettle'. I had misspelt it. The teacher tried to prompt me with the point of his boot, but I would not be prompted. It was beyond me to see that he wanted me to copy the spelling from my neighbour's slate, for I had thought that the teacher was there to supervise us against copying. The result was that all the boys, except myself, were found to have spelt every word correctly. Only I had been stupid. The teacher tried later to tell me that I should not have been so stupid, but without effect. I never could learn the art of 'copying'.

Yet the incident did not in the least lessen my respect for my teacher. I was, by nature, blind to the faults of elders. Later I came to know of many other failings of this teacher, but my regard for him remained the same. For I had learnt to carry out the orders of elders, not to look critically at their actions.

Two other incidents belonging to the same period have always clung to my memory. As a rule I did not like any reading beyond my school books. The daily lessons had to be done, because I did not want to be taken to task by my teacher, nor to deceive him. Therefore, I would do the lessons, but often without my mind in them. Thus when even the lessons could not be done properly, there was of course no question of any extra reading. But somehow my eyes fell on a book purchased by my father. It was *Shravana*[1] *Pitribhakti Nataka* (a play about Shravana's devotion to his parents). I read it with intense interest. There came to our place about the same time wandering showmen. One of the pictures I was shown was of Shravana carrying, by means of slings fitted for his shoulders, his blind parents on a pilgrimage. The book and the picture left a permanent impression on my mind. 'Here is an example for you to copy,' I said to myself.

---

1 Shravana, a young ascetic, was extremely devoted to his blind parents whom he carried in a hammock for a pilgrimage. On his way he was accidentally shot dead by Rama's father, King Dasharatha.

Just about this time, I had secured my father's permission to see a play performed by a certain dramatic company. This play—*Harishchandra*[2]—captured my heart. I could never be tired of seeing it. But how often should I be permitted to go? I kept thinking about it all the time and I must have acted Harishchandra to myself times without number. 'Why should not all be truthful like Harishchandra?' was the question I asked myself day and night. To follow truth and to go through all the ordeals Harishchandra went through was the one ideal it inspired in me. I literally believed in the story of Harishchandra. The thought of it all often made me weep.

I was not regarded as a dunce at the high school. I always enjoyed the affection of my teachers. Certificates of progress and character used to be sent to the parents every year. I never had a bad certificate. In fact, I even won prizes after I passed out of the second standard. In the fifth and sixth I obtained scholarships of rupees four and ten respectively, an achievement for which I have to thank good luck more than my merit. For the scholarships were not open to all, but reserved for the best boys amongst those coming from the Sorath Division of Kathiawad. And in those days there could

---

2 Harishchandra, according to Hindu epics, was a king. He was famous for his liberality, and unflinching adherence to truth. The celebrated sage Vishwamitra decided to test the king and subjected him to very severe tests including compulsion to put his own wife to death as a witch! The king, however, stood the test with great courage and truthfulness.

not have been many boys from Sorath in a class of forty to fifty.

My own recollection is that I had not any high regard for my ability. I used to be astonished whenever I won prizes and scholarships. But I very jealously guarded my character. The least little fault drew tears from my eyes. When I merited, or seemed to the teacher to merit, a rebuke, it was unbearable for me. I remember having once received a beating. I did not so much mind the punishment, as the fact that it was considered my deserts. I wept piteously. That was when I was in the first or second standard. There was another such incident during the time when I was in the seventh standard. Dorabji Edulji Gimi was the headmaster then. He was popular among boys, as he was a disciplinarian, a man of method and a good teacher. He had made gymnastics and cricket compulsory for boys of the upper standards. I disliked both. I never took part in any exercise, cricket or football, before they were made compulsory. My shyness was one of the reasons for this aloofness, which I now see was wrong. I then had the false notion that gymnastics had nothing to do with education.

I may mention, however, that I was none the worse for keeping away from exercise. That was because I had read in books about the benefits of long walks in the open air, and having liked the advice, I had formed a habit of taking walks, which has still remained with me. These walks gave me a fairly hardy constitution.

The reason of my dislike for gymnastics was my keen desire to serve as nurse to my father. As soon as the school closed, I would hurry home and begin serving him. Compulsory exercise came directly in the way of this service. I requested Mr Gimi to exempt me from gymnastics so that I might be free to serve my father. But he would not listen to me. Now it so happened that one Saturday, when we had school in the morning, I had to go from home to the school for gymnastics at 4 o'clock in the afternoon. I had no watch, and the clouds deceived me. Before I reached the school the boys had all left. The next day Mr Gimi, examining the roll, found me marked absent. Being asked the reason for absence, I told him what had happened. He refused to believe me and ordered me to pay a fine of one or two annas (I cannot now recall how much).

I was convicted of lying! That deeply pained me. How was I to prove my innocence? There was no way. I cried in deep anguish. I saw that a man of truth must also be a man of care. This was the first and last instance of my carelessness in school. I have a faint recollection that I finally succeeded in getting the fine refunded. The exemption from exercise was of course obtained, as my father wrote himself to the headmaster saying that he wanted me at home after school.

But though I was none the worse for having neglected exercise, I am still paying the penalty of another neglect. I do not know whence I got the notion that good handwriting was not a necessary part of education, but I retained it until I went to England. Bad handwriting should be regarded as a sign of an imperfect education. I tried later to improve mine, but it was too late. I could never repair the neglect of my youth.

Two more incidents of my school days are worth recording. I had lost one year because of my marriage, and the teacher wanted me to make good the loss by skipping the class – a privilege usually allowed to hard-working boys. I therefore had only six months in the third standard and was promoted to the fourth after the examinations which are followed by the summer vacation. Most subjects were taught in English from the fourth standard. I found it very hard. Geometry was a new subject in which I was not particularly strong, and the English medium made it still more difficult for me. The teacher taught the subject very well but I could not follow him. Often I would lose heart and think of going back to the third standard, feeling that the packing of two years' studies into a single year was too much. But this would discredit not only me, but also the teacher; because, counting on my ability, he had recommended my promotion. So the fear of the double discredit kept me at my post. When, however, with much effort I reached the thirteenth proposition of Euclid, the utter simplicity of the subject became clear to me. A subject which only required a pure and simple use of one's reasoning powers could not be difficult. Ever since that time geometry has been both easy and interesting for me.

Sanskrit, however, proved a harder task. In geometry there was nothing to memorize, whereas in Sanskrit, I thought, everything had to be learnt by heart. This subject also began from the fourth standard. As soon as I entered the sixth I became disheartened. The teacher was a hard task-master, anxious, as I thought, to force the boys. There was a sort of rivalry going on between the Sanskrit and the Persian teachers. The Persian teacher was lenient. The boys used to talk among themselves that Persian was very easy and the Persian teacher very good

CHILDHOOD AND YOUTH

and considerate to the students. The 'easiness' tempted me and one day I sat in the Persian class. The Sanskrit teacher was grieved. He called me to his side and said: 'How can you forget that you are the son of a Vaishnava father? Won't you learn the language of your own religion? If you have any difficulty, why not come to me? I want to teach you students Sanskrit to the best of my ability. As you proceed further, you will find in it things of great interest. You should not lose heart. Come and sit again in the Sanskrit class.'

This kindness put me to shame. I could not disregard my teacher's affection. If I had not acquired the little Sanskrit that I learnt then, I should have found it difficult to take any interest in our sacred books. In fact I am sorry now that I was not able to acquire a more thorough knowledge of the language, because I have since realized that every Hindu boy and girl should possess sound Sanskrit learning.

Marriage

It is my painful duty to have to record here my marriage at the age of thirteen. As I see the youngsters of the same age about me who are under my care, and think of my own marriage, I am inclined to pity myself and to congratulate them on having escaped my lot. I can see no moral argument in support of such early marriage.

I do not think it meant to me anything more than good clothes to wear, drum beating, marriage processions, rich dinners and a strange girl to play with. We gradually began to know each other, and to speak freely together. We were the same age. But I took no time in assuming the authority of a husband.

I would not allow my wife to go anywhere without my permission. And Kasturba was not the girl to put up with any such thing. She made it a point to go out whenever and wherever she liked. More restraint on my part resulted in more liberty being taken by her and in my getting more and more angry. Refusal to speak to one another thus became the order of the day with us, married children. I think it was quite innocent of Kasturba not to have bothered about my restrictions. How could an innocent girl put up with any restraint on going to the temple or on going on visits to friends? If I had the right to restrict her, had not she also a similar right? All this is clear to me today. But at that time I had to make good my authority as a husband!

Let not the reader think, however, that ours was a life of constant quarrels. For my severities were all based on love. I wanted to make my wife an ideal wife. My ambition was to make her live a pure life, learn what I learnt, and identify her life and thought with mine.

I do not think Kasturba had any such desire. She did not know to read or write. By nature she was simple, independent, persevering and, with me at least, shy. She was not impatient of her ignorance and I do not recollect my studies having ever made her want to go in for studies herself.

A Tragic Friendship

Amongst my few friends at the high school I had, at different times, two who might be called intimate. One of these friendships did not last long, though I never gave up my friend. He gave me up, because I made friends with the other. This latter friendship I regard as a tragedy in my life. It lasted long. I formed it in the spirit of a reformer.

This companion was originally my elder brother's friend. They were classmates. I knew his weaknesses, but I regarded him as a faithful friend. My mother, my eldest brother, and my wife warned me that I was in bad company. I was too proud to heed my wife's warning. But I dared not go against the opinion of my mother and my eldest brother. Nevertheless, I pleaded with them, saying, 'I know he has the weakness you attribute to him but you do not know his virtues. He cannot lead me astray, as my association with him is meant to reform him. For I am sure that if he reforms his ways, he will be a splendid man. I beg you not to be anxious on my account.'

I do not think this satisfied them, but they accepted my explanation and let me go my way.

A wave of 'reform' was sweeping over Rajkot at the time when I first came across this friend. He informed me that many of our teachers were secretly taking meat and wine. He also named many well-known people of Rajkot as belonging to the same company. There were also, I was told, some high school boys among them.

I was surprised and pained. I asked my friend the reason and he explained it thus: 'We are a weak people because we do not eat meat. The English are able to rule over us, because they are meat-eaters. You know how hardy I am, and how great a runner too. It is because I am a meat-eater. Meat-eaters do not have boils, and even if they sometimes happen to have any, these heal quickly. Our teachers and other distinguished people who eat meat are no fools. They know its virtues. You should do likewise. There is nothing like trying. Try, and see what strength it gives.'

All these pleas on behalf of meat-eating were not made at a single sitting. They represent the substance of a long and elaborate argument which my friend was trying to impress upon me from time to time. My elder brother had already fallen. He therefore supported my friend's argument. I certainly looked feeble-bodied by the side of my brother and this friend. They were both hardier, physically stronger, and more daring. This friend's exploits cast a spell over me. He could run long distances and extraordinarily fast. He was an adept in high and long jumping. He could put up with any amount of physical punishment. He would often display his exploits to me and as one is always dazzled when he sees in others the qualities that he lacks himself, I was dazzled by this friend's exploits. This was followed by a strong desire to be like him. I could hardly jump or run. Why should not I also be as strong as he?

Moreover, I was a coward. I used to be afraid of thieves, ghosts and serpents. I did not dare to stir out of doors at night. Darkness was a terror to me. It was almost impossible for me to sleep in the dark, as I would imagine ghosts coming from one direction, thieves from another and serpents from a third. I could not therefore bear to sleep without a light in the room. My friend knew all these weaknesses of mine. He would tell me that he could hold in his hand live serpents, could defy thieves and did not believe in ghosts.

All these had its due effect on me. I was beaten. It began to grow on me that meat-eating was good, that it would make me strong and daring, and that, if the whole country took to meat-eating, the English could be overcome.

A day was thereupon fixed for beginning the experiment. It had to be done in secret as my parents were orthodox Vaishnavas, and I was extremely devoted to them. I cannot say that I did not know then that I should have to deceive my parents if I began eating meat. But my mind was bent on the 'reform'. It was not a question of having something tasty to eat. I did not know that it had a particularly good taste. I wished to be strong and daring and wanted my countrymen also to be such. The zeal for the 'reform' blinded me. And having ensured secrecy, I persuaded myself that mere hiding the deed from parents was no departure from truth.

So the day came. We went in search of a lonely spot by the river, and there I saw, for the first time, in my life, meat. There was baker's bread also. I did not like either. The goat's meat was as tough as leather. I simply could not eat it. I was sick and had to leave off eating.

I had a very bad night afterwards. A horrible dream haunted me. Every time I dropped off to sleep it would seem as though a live goat were crying inside me, and I would jump up sorry for what I had done. But then I would remind myself that meat-eating was a duty and so become more cheerful.

My friend was not a man to give in easily. He now began to cook various delicacies with meat. And for dining, no longer was the quiet spot on the river chosen, but a State house, with its dining hall and tables and chairs, about which my friend had made arrangements with the chief cook there.

Gradually I got over my dislike for bread, gave up my pity for the goats, and began to enjoy meat-dishes, if not meat itself. This went on for about a year. But not more than half a dozen meat-feasts were enjoyed in all. I had no money to pay for this 'reform'. My friend had therefore always to find the money. I had no knowledge where he found it. But find it he did, because he was bent on turning me into a meat-eater. But even his means must have been limited, and hence these feasts had necessarily to be few and far between.

Whenever I had occasion to indulge in these secret feasts, eating at home was impossible. My mother would naturally ask me to come and take my food and want to know the reason why I did not wish to eat. I would say to her, 'I have no appetite today; there is something wrong with my digestion.' I knew I was lying, and lying to my mother. I also knew that, if my mother and father came to know of my having become a meat-eater, they would be deeply shocked. This knowledge was making me feel uneasy.

Therefore I said to myself: 'Though it is essential to eat meat, and also essential to take up food "reform" in the country, yet deceiving and lying to one's father and mother is worse than not eating meat. In their lifetime, therefore, meat-eating must be given up. When they are no more and I have found my freedom, I will eat meat openly, but until that moment arrives I will keep away from it.'

This decision I told to my friend, and I have never since gone back to meat.

Stealing

I have still to relate some of my failings during this meat-eating period and also previous to it, which date from before my marriage or soon after.

A relative and I became fond of smoking. Not that we saw any good in smoking, or liked the smell of a cigarette. We simply imagined a sort of pleasure in sending out clouds of smoke from our mouths. My uncle had the habit, and we should copy his example. But we had no money. So we began stealing stumps of cigarettes thrown away by my uncle.

The stumps, however, were not always available, and could not give out much smoke either. So we began to steal coppers from the servant's pocket-money in order to purchase Indian cigarettes. But the question was where to keep them. We could not of course smoke in the presence of elders. We managed somehow for a few weeks on these stolen coppers. In the meantime we heard that the stalks of a certain plant could be smoked like cigarettes. We got them and began this kind of smoking.

But we were far from being satisfied with such things as these. Our want of independence began to be painful. It was unbearable that we should be unable to do anything without the elders' permission. At last, in sheer disgust, we decided to commit suicide!

But how were we to do it? From where were we to get the poison? We heard that *dhatura* seeds were an effective poison. Off we went to the jungle in search of these seeds and got them. Evening was thought to be the auspicious hour. We went to Kedarji Mandir, put ghee in the temple-lamp, had the *darshan* and then looked for a lonely corner. But our courage failed us. Supposing we were not at once killed? And what was the good of killing ourselves? Why not rather put up with the lack of independence? But we swallowed two or three seeds nevertheless. We dared not take more. Both of us did not like to die, and decided to go to Ramji Mandir to calm ourselves, and to dismiss the thought of suicide.

I realized that it was not easy to commit suicide.

The thought of suicide ultimately resulted in both of us bidding goodbye to the habit of smoking and of stealing the servant's coppers for the purpose.

Ever since I have grown up, I have never desired to smoke and have always regarded the habit of smoking as barbarous, dirty and harmful. I have never understood why there is such a desire for smoking throughout the world. I cannot bear to travel in a compartment full of people smoking. I become choked.

But much more serious than this theft was the one I was guilty of a little later. I stole the coppers when I was twelve or thirteen, possibly less. The other theft was committed when I was fifteen. In this case I stole a bit of gold out of my meat-eating brother's armlet. This brother had run into a debt of about twenty-five rupees. He had on his arm an armlet of solid gold. It was not difficult to clip a bit out of it.

Well, it was done, and the debt cleared. But this became more than I could bear. I resolved never to steal again. I also made up my mind to confess it to my father. But I did not

CHILDHOOD AND YOUTH

dare to speak. Not that I was afraid of my father beating me. No. I do not recall his ever having beaten any of us. I was afraid of the pain that I should cause him. But I felt that the risk should be taken; that there could not be cleansing without a clean confession.

I decided at last to write out the confession to submit it to my father, and ask his forgiveness. I wrote it on a slip of paper and handed it to him myself. In this note not only did I confess my guilt, but I asked adequate punishment for it, and closed with a request to him not to punish himself for my offence. I also pledged myself never to steal in future.

I was trembling as I handed the confession to my father. He was then confined to bed. His bed was a plain wooden plank. I handed him the note and sat opposite the plank.

He read it through, and tears trickled down his cheeks, wetting the paper. For a moment he closed his eyes in thought and then tore up the note. He had sat up to read it. He again lay down. I also cried. I could see my father's agony. If I were a painter I could draw a picture of the whole scene today. It is still so vivid in my mind.

Those tears of love cleansed my heart, and washed my sin away. Only he who has experienced such love can know what it is.

This sort of forgiveness was not natural to my father. I had thought that he would be angry, say hard things, and strike his forehead. But he was so wonderfully peaceful, and I believe this was due to my clean confession. A clean confession, combined with a promise never to commit the sin again, when offered before one who has the right to receive it, is the purest type of repentance. I know that my confession made my father feel absolutely safe about me, and increased greatly his affection for me.

My Father's Illness and Death

The time of which I am now speaking is my sixteenth year. My father, as we have seen, was bed-ridden. My mother, an old servant of the house, and I were attending on him. I had the duties of a nurse, which mainly consisted in dressing the wound, and giving my father his medicine. Every night I massaged his legs and retired only when he asked me to do so or after he had fallen asleep. I loved to do this service. I do not remember ever having neglected it. All the time at my disposal, after the performance of the daily duties, was divided between school and attending on my father. I would only go out for an evening walk either when he permitted me or when he was feeling well.

The dreadful night came. It was 10:30 or 11 p.m. I was giving the massage. My uncle offered to relieve me. I was glad and went straight to bed. In five or six minutes, however, the servant knocked at the door. I started with alarm. 'Get up,' he said. 'Father is very ill.' I knew of course that he was very ill, and so I guessed what 'very ill' meant at that moment. I sprang out of bed.

'What is the matter? Do tell me!'

'Father is no more.'

So all was over! I felt very unhappy that I was not near my father when he died.

Glimpses of Religion

I have said before that there was in me a fear of ghosts and spirits. Rambha, my nurse, suggested, as a remedy for this fear, the repetition of *Ramanama* or the name of God. I had more faith in her than in her remedy, and so at a very early age began repeating *Ramanama* to cure my fear of ghosts and spirits. This was of course short-lived, but the good seed sown in childhood was not sown in vain. I think it is due to the seed sown by that good woman Rambha that today *Ramanama* is a never-failing remedy for me.

During part of his illness, my father was in Porbandar. There every evening he used to listen to the *Ramayana*. The reader was a great devotee of Rama. He had a good voice. He would sing the verses and explain them, losing himself in the story and carrying his listeners along with him. I must have been thirteen at that time, but I remember being quite taken up by his reading. That laid the foundation of my deep devotion to the *Ramayana*. Today I regard the *Ramayana* of Tulsidas as the greatest book in all religious literature.

In Rajkot I learnt to be friendly to all branches of Hinduism and sister religions. For my father and mother would visit the Haveli as also Shiva's and Rama's temples, and would take or send us youngsters there. Jain monks also would pay frequent visits to my father, and would even go out of their way to accept food from us – non-Jains. They would have talks with my father on subjects religious and worldly.

He had besides, Mussalman and Parsi friends, who would talk to him about their own faiths, and he would listen to them always with respect, and often with interest. Being his nurse, I often had a chance to be present at these talks. These many things combined to teach me toleration for all faiths.

Only Christianity was at the time an exception. I developed a sort of dislike for it. And for a reason. In those days Christian missionaries used to stand in a corner near the high school and preach against Hindus and their gods. I could not endure this. About the same time, I heard of a well-known Hindu having been converted to Christianity. It was the talk of the town that when he was baptized, he had to eat beef and drink liquor, that he also had to change his clothes, and that from then on he began to go about in European costume including a hat. I also heard that the new convert had already begun abusing the religion of his ancestors, their customs and their country. All these things made me dislike Christianity.

But the fact that I had learnt to be tolerant to other religions did not mean that I had any living faith in God. But one thing took deep root in me – the conviction that morality is the basis of things and that truth is the substance of all morality.

A Gujarati verse likewise gripped my mind and heart. Its teaching—return good for evil—became my guiding principle. It became such a passion with me that I began numerous experiments in it. Here are those (for me) wonderful lines:

> For a bowl of water give a goodly meal;
> For a kindly greeting bow thou down with zeal;
> For a simple penny pay thou back with gold;
> If thy life be rescued, life do not withhold.

Thus the words and actions of the wise regard;
Every little service tenfold they reward.
But the truly noble know all men as one
And return with gladness good for evil done.

Preparation for England

My elders wanted me to continue my studies at college after school. There was a college in Bhavnagar as well as in Bombay, and as the former was cheaper, I decided to go there and join the Samaldas College. I went, but found everything very difficult. At the end of the first term, I returned home.

We had in Mavji Dave, who was a shrewd and learned Brahman, an old friend and adviser of the family. He had kept up his connection with the family even after my father's death. He happened to visit us during my holidays. In conversation with my mother and elder brother, he inquired about my studies. Learning that I was at Samaldas College, he said: 'The times are changed. And none of you can expect to succeed to your father's *gadi* (official work) without having had a proper education. Now as this boy is still pursuing his studies, you should all look to him to keep the *gadi*. It will take him four or five years to get his B.A. degree, which will at best qualify him for a sixty rupees' post, not for a Diwanship. If like my son he went in for law, it would take him still longer, by which time there would be a host of lawyers aspiring for a Diwan's post. I would far rather that you sent him to England. Think of that barrister who has just come back from England. How stylishly he lives! He could get the Diwanship for the asking. I would strongly advise you to send Mohandas to England this very year. Kevalram has numerous friends in England. He will give notes of introduction to them, and Mohandas will have an easy time of it there.'

Joshiji—that is how we used to call old Mavji Dave—turned to me and asked: 'Would you not rather go to England than study here?' Nothing could have been more welcome to me. I was finding my studies difficult. So I jumped at the proposal and said that the sooner I was sent the better. My elder brother was greatly troubled in his mind. How was he to find the money to send me? And was it proper to trust a young man like me to go abroad alone? My mother was very worried. She did not like the idea of parting with me. She had begun making minute inquiries. Someone had told her that young men got lost in England. Someone else had said that they took to meat; and yet another that they could not live there without liquor. 'How about all this?' she asked me. I said: 'Will you not trust me? I shall not lie to you. I promise that I shall not touch any of those things. If there were any such danger, would Joshiji let me go?'

'I can trust you,' she said. 'But how can I trust you in a distant land? I am confused and know not what to do. I will ask Becharji Swami.'

Becharji Swami was originally a Modh Bania, but had now become a Jain monk. He too was a family adviser like Joshiji. He came to my help, and said: 'I shall get the boy solemnly to take the three vows, and then he can be allowed to go.' I vowed not to touch wine, woman and meat. This done, my mother gave her permission.

The high school had a send-off in my honour. It was an uncommon thing for a young man of Rajkot to go to England. I had written out a few words of thanks. But I could scarcely read them out. I remember how my head reeled and how my whole frame shook as I stood up to read them.

With my mother's permission and blessings, I set off happily for Bombay, leaving my wife with a baby of a few months. But on arrival there friends told my brother that the Indian Ocean was rough in June and July, and as this was my first voyage, I should not be allowed to sail until November.

Meanwhile my caste-people were agitated over my going abroad. A general meeting of the caste was called and I was summoned to appear before it. I went. How I suddenly managed to gather up courage I do not know. Fearless, and without the slightest hesitation, I came before the meeting. The Sheth—the headman of the community—who was distantly related to me and had been on very good terms with my father, thus spoke to me:

'In the opinion of the caste your proposal to go to England is not proper. Our religion forbids voyages abroad. We have also heard that it is not possible to live there and keep to our religion. One is obliged to eat and drink with Europeans!'

To which I replied: 'I do not think it is at all against our religion to go to England. I intend going there for further studies. And I have already solemnly promised to my mother to keep away from three things you fear most. I am sure the vow will keep me safe.'

'But we tell you,' replied the Sheth, 'that it is not possible to keep our religion there. You know my relations with your father and you ought to listen to my advice.'

'I know those relations,' said I. 'And you are as an elder to me. But I am helpless in this matter. I cannot change my decisions to go to England. My father's friend and adviser, who is a learned Brahman sees no objection to my going to England, and my mother and brother have also given me their permission.'

'But will you disregard the orders of the caste?'

'I am really helpless. I think the caste should not interfere in the matter.'

This made the Sheth very angry. He swore at me. I sat unmoved. So the Sheth ordered: 'This boy shall be treated as an outcaste from today. Whoever helps him or goes to see him off at dock shall be punishable with a fine of one rupee four annas.'

The order had no effect on me, and I took my leave of the Sheth. But I wondered how my brother would take it. Fortunately, he remained firm and wrote to assure me that I had his permission to go, in spite of the Sheth's order.

A berth was reserved for me by my friends in the same cabin as that of Shri Tryambakrai Mazmudar, the Junagadh Vakil. They also asked him to help me. He was an experienced man of mature age and knew the world. I was yet a youth of eighteen without any experience of the world. Shri Mazmudar told my friends not to worry about me.

I sailed at last from Bombay on the 4th of September.

On Board the Ship

I was not used to talking English, and except for Shri Mazmudar all the other passengers in the second saloon were English. I could not speak to them. For I could rarely follow their remarks when they came up to speak to me, and even when I understood I could not reply. I had to frame every sentence in my mind before I could bring it out. I was innocent of the use of knives and forks and had not the boldness to inquire what dishes on the menu were free of meat. I therefore never took meals at table but always had them in my cabin, and they consisted principally of sweets and fruits which I had brought with me. Shri Mazmudar had no difficulty, and he mixed with everybody. He would move about freely on deck, while I hid myself in the cabin the whole day, only going up on deck when there were but few people. Shri Mazmudar kept pleading with me to associate with the passengers and to talk with them freely. He told me that lawyers should have a long tongue, and related to me his legal experience. He advised me to take every possible opportunity of talking English and not to mind making mistakes which were obviously unavoidable with a foreign tongue. But nothing could make me conquer my shyness.

An English passenger, wanting to be nice to me, drew me into conversation. He was older than I. He asked me what I ate, what I was, where I was going, why I was shy, and so on. He also advised me to come to table. He laughed at my insistence on not eating meat, and said in a friendly way when we were in the Red Sea: 'It is all very well so far but you will have to change your decision in the Bay of Biscay. And it is so cold in England that one cannot possibly live there without meat.'

'But I have heard that people can live there without eating meat,' I said.

'Rest assured it is a lie,' said he. 'No one, to my knowledge, lives there without being a meat-eater. Don't you see that I am not asking you to take liquor, though I do so? But I do think you should eat meat, for you cannot live without it.'

'I thank you for your kind advice, but I have solemnly promised to my mother not to touch meat, and therefore I cannot think of taking it. If it be found impossible to get on without it, I will far rather go back to India than eat meat in order to remain there.'

We entered the Bay of Biscay, but I did not begin to feel the need either of meat or liquor. We reached Southampton, as far as I remember, on a Saturday. On the boat I had worn a black suit, the white flannel one, which my friends had got me, having been kept especially for wearing when I landed. I had thought that white clothes would suit me better when I stepped ashore, and therefore, I did so in white flannels. Those were the last days of September, and I found I was the only person wearing such clothes. I left in charge of an agent of Grindlay and Co. all my luggage including the keys, seeing that many others had done the same and I thought I must do like them.

Someone on board had advised us to put up at the Victoria Hotel in London. Shri Mazmudar and I accordingly went there. The shame of being the only person in white clothes was already too much for me. And when at the Hotel I was told that I should not get my things from Grindlay's the next day, it being a Sunday, I felt very bad.

Dr Mehta to whom I had wired from Southampton, called at about eight o'clock the same evening. He gave me a hearty greeting. He smiled at my being in white flannels. As we were talking, I casually picked up his top hat, and trying to see how smooth it was, passed my hand over it the wrong way and disturbed the fur. Dr Mehta looked somewhat angrily at what I was doing and stopped me. But the mischief had been done. The incident was a warning for the future, and Dr Mehta gave me my first lesson in European etiquette. 'Do not touch other people's things,' he said. 'Do not ask questions as we usually do in India on first acquaintance; do not talk loudly; never address people as "sir" whilst speaking to them as we do in India; only servants and subordinates address their masters that way.' And so on and so forth. He also told me that it was very expensive to live in a hotel and recommended that I should live with a private family.

Shri Mazmudar and I found the hotel to be a trying affair. It was also very expensive. There was, however, a Sindhi fellow-passenger from Malta who had become friends with Shri Mazmudar, and as he was not a stranger to London, he offered to find rooms for us. We agreed, and on Monday, as soon as we got our baggage, we paid up our bills and went to the rooms rented for us by the Sindhi friend. I remember my hotel bill came to £3, an amount which shocked me. And I had practically starved in spite of this heavy bill! For I could relish nothing. When I did not like one thing, I asked for another, but had to pay for both just the same. The fact is that all this while I had depended on the foodstuffs which I had brought with me from Bombay.

I was very uneasy even in the new rooms. I would continually think of my home and country, and of my mother's love. At night the tears would stream down my cheeks, and home memories of all sorts made sleep out of the question. It was impossible to share my misery with anyone. And even if I could have done so, where was the use? I knew of nothing that would soothe me. Everything was strange – the people, their ways, and even their dwellings. I was a complete stranger to English etiquette and continually had to be on my guard. There was the additional inconvenience of the vegetarian vow. Even the dishes that I could eat were tasteless. I thus found myself between Scylla and Charybdis.[3] England I could not bear, but to return to India was not to be thought of. Now that I had come, I must finish the three years, said the inner voice.

---

3 Scylla is a monster, according to Greek legend, living on the Italian side of the Straits of Messina, and opposite to it is Charybdis, a whirlpool. So the phrase means being faced with two equally unpleasant alternatives. – Ed.

In England as a Student

In London

Dr Mehta went on Monday to the Victoria Hotel expecting to find me there. He discovered that we had left, got our new address, and met me at our rooms. Dr Mehta inspected my room and its furniture and shook his head in disapproval. 'This place won't do,' he said. 'We come to England not so much for the purpose of studies as for gaining experience of English life and customs. And for this you need to live with a family. But before you do so, I think you had better be for a period with —. I will take you there.'

I gratefully accepted the suggestion and removed to the friend's rooms. He was all kindness and attention. He treated me as his own brother, initiated me into English ways and manners, and accustomed me to talking the language. My food, however, became a serious question. I could not relish boiled vegetables cooked without salt or spices. The landlady was at a loss to know what to prepare for me. We had oatmeal porridge for breakfast, which was fairly filling, but I always starved at lunch and dinner. The friend continually reasoned with me to eat meat, but I always pleaded my vow and then remained silent. Both for luncheon and dinner we had spinach and bread and jam too. I was a good eater and had a big appetite; but I was ashamed to ask for more than two or three slices of bread, as it did not seem correct to do so. Added to this, there was no milk either for lunch or dinner. The friend once got disgusted with this state of things, and said: 'Had you been my own brother, I would have sent you away. What is the value of a vow made before an illiterate mother and in ignorance of conditions here? It is no vow at all. It would not be regarded as a vow in law. It is pure superstition to stick to such a promise. And I tell you this persistence will not help you to gain anything here. You confess to having eaten and liked meat. You took it where it was absolutely unnecessary, and will not where it is quite essential. What a pity!'

But I was unyielding.

Day in and day out the friend would argue, but I had an eternal no to face him with. The more he argued, the firmer I became. Daily I would pray for God's protection and get it. Not that I had any idea of God. It was faith that was at work – faith of which the seed had been sown by the good nurse Rambha.

I had not yet started upon regular studies. In India I had never read a newspaper. But here I succeeded in cultivating a liking for them by regular reading. This took me hardly an hour. I therefore began to wander about. I went out in search of a vegetarian restaurant. I hit on one in Farringdon Street. The sight of it filled me with the same joy that a child feels on getting a thing after its own heart. Before I entered I noticed books for sale exhibited under a glass window near the door. I saw among them Salt's *Plea for Vegetarianism*. This I purchased for a shilling and went straight to the dining room. This was my first hearty meal since my arrival in England. God had come to my aid.

I read Salt's book from cover to cover and was very much impressed by it. From the date of reading this book, I may claim to have become a vegetarian by choice. I blessed the day on which I had taken the vow before my mother. The choice was now made in favour of vegetarianism, the spread of which henceforward became my mission.

Playing the English Gentleman

Meanwhile, my friend had not ceased to worry about me. One day, he invited me to go to the theatre. Before the play we were to dine together at the Holborn Restaurant. The friend had planned to take me to this restaurant evidently imagining that modesty would prevent me from asking any questions. And it was a very big company of diners in the midst of which my friend and I sat sharing a table between us. The first course was soup. I wondered what it might be made of, but did not dare ask the friend about it. I therefore summoned the waiter. My friend saw the movement and sternly asked across the table what was the matter. With considerable hesitation I told him that I wanted to inquire if the soup was a vegetable soup. 'You are too clumsy for decent society,' he angrily exclaimed. 'If you cannot behave yourself, you had better go. Feed in some other restaurant and await me outside.' This delighted me. Out I went. There was a vegetarian restaurant close by, but it was closed. So I went without food that night. I accompanied my friend to the theatre, but he never said a word about the scene I had created. On my part of course there was nothing to say.

That was the last friendly quarrel we had. It did not affect our relations in the least. I could see and appreciate the love underlying all my friend's efforts, and my respect for him was all the greater on account of our differences in thought and action.

But I decided that I should put him at ease, that I should assure him that I would be clumsy no more, but try to become polished and make up for my vegetarianism by cultivating other accomplishments which fitted one for polite society. And for this purpose I undertook the all too impossible task of becoming an English gentleman.

The clothes after the Bombay cut that I was wearing were, I thought, unsuitable for English society, and I got new ones at the Army and Navy Stores. I also went in for a chimney-pot hat costing nineteen shillings – an excessive price in those days. Not content with this, I wasted ten pounds on an evening suit made in Bond Street, the centre of fashionable life in London; and got my good and noble-hearted brother to send me a double watch chain of gold. It was not correct to wear a ready-made tie and I learnt the art of tying one for myself. While in India the mirror had been a luxury permitted on the days when the family barber gave me a shave. Here I wasted ten minutes every day before a

IN ENGLAND AS A STUDENT

huge mirror, watching myself arranging my tie and parting my hair in the correct fashion. My hair was by no means soft, and every day it meant a regular struggle with the brush to keep it in position. Each time the hat was put on and off, the hand would automatically move towards the head to adjust the hair, not to mention the other civilized habit of the hand every now and then doing the same thing when sitting in polished society.

As if all this were not enough to make me look the thing, I directed my attention to other details that were supposed to go towards the making of an English gentleman. I was told it was necessary for me to take lessons in dancing, French, and elocution or speechmaking. French was not only the language of neighbouring France, but it was a language understood all over Europe where I had a desire to travel. I decided to take dancing lessons at a class and paid down £3 as fees for a term. I must have taken about six lessons in three weeks. But it was beyond me to achieve anything like rhythmic motion. I could not follow the piano and hence found it impossible to keep time. What then was I to do? The recluse in the fable kept a cat to keep off the rats, and then a cow to feed the cat with milk, and a man to keep the cow and so on. My ambitions also grew like the family of the recluse. I thought I should learn to play the violin in order to cultivate an ear for Western music. So I invested £3 in a violin and something more in fees. I sought a third teacher to give me lessons in elocution and paid him a preliminary fee of a guinea. He recommended Bell's *Standard Elocutionist* as the text book, which I purchased. And I began with a speech of Pitt's.

But soon I began to ask myself what the purpose of all this was.

I had not to spend a lifetime in England, I said to myself. What then was the use of learning elocution? And how could dancing make a gentleman of me? The violin I could learn even in India. I was a student and ought to go on with my studies. I should qualify myself to become a barrister. If my character made a gentleman of me, so much the better. Otherwise I should give up the ambition.

These and similar thoughts possessed me, and I expressed them in a letter which I addressed to the elocution teacher, requesting him to excuse me from further lessons. I had taken only two or three. I wrote a similar letter to the dancing teacher, and went personally to the violin teacher with a request to dispose of the violin for any price it might fetch. She was rather friendly to me, so I told her how I had discovered that I was pursuing a false idea. She encouraged me in my decision to make a complete change.

This infatuation must have lasted about three months. Being particular about dress persisted for years. But henceforward I became a student.

Changes

Let no one imagine that my experiments in dancing and the like marked a stage of indulgence in my life. The reader will have noticed that even then I knew what I was doing and my expenses were carefully calculated.

As I kept strict watch over my way of living, I could see that it was necessary to economize. So I decided to take rooms

IN ENGLAND AS A STUDENT

on my own account, instead of living any longer in a family, and also to remove from place to place according to the work I had to do, thus gaining experience at the same time. The rooms were so selected as to enable me to reach the place of business on foot in half an hour, and so save fares. Before this I had always taken some kind of conveyance whenever I went anywhere, and had to find extra time for walks. The new arrangement combined walks and economy, as it meant a saving of fares and gave me walks of eight or ten miles a day. It was mainly this habit of long walks that kept me practically free from illness throughout my stay in England and gave me a fairly strong body.

Thus I rented a suite of rooms; one for a sitting room and another for a bedroom. This was the second stage. The third was yet to come.

These changes saved me half the expenses. But how was I to utilize the time? I knew that Bar examinations did not require much study, and I therefore did not feel pressed for time. My weak English was a perpetual worry to me. I should, I thought, not only be called to the Bar, but have some literary degree as well. I inquired about the Oxford and Cambridge University courses, consulted a few friends, and found that, if I elected to go to either of these places, that would mean greater expense and a much longer stay in England than I was prepared for. A friend suggested that, if I really wanted to have the satisfaction of taking a difficult examination, I should pass the London Matriculation. It meant a good deal of labour and much addition to my stock of general knowledge, without any extra expense worth the name. I welcomed the suggestion. But the syllabus frightened me. Latin and a modern language were compulsory! How was I to manage Latin? But the friend entered a strong plea for it: 'Latin is very valuable to lawyers. Knowledge of Latin is very useful in understanding law books. And one paper in Roman Law is entirely in Latin. Besides a knowledge of Latin means greater command over the English language.' This appealed to me and I decided to learn Latin, no matter how difficult it might be. French I had already begun, so I thought that should be the modern language. I joined a private Matriculation class. Examinations were held every six months and I had only five months at my disposal. It was an almost impossible task for me. I converted myself into a serious student. I framed my own timetable to the minute; but neither my intelligence nor memory promised to enable me to tackle Latin and French besides other subjects within the given period. The result was that I failed in Latin. I was sorry but did not lose heart. I had acquired a taste for Latin, also I thought my French would be all the better for another trial and I would select a new subject in the science group. Chemistry which was my subject in science had no attraction for want of experiments, whereas it ought to have been a deeply interesting study. It was one of the compulsory subjects in India and so I had selected it for the London Matriculation. This time, however, I chose Heat and Light instead of Chemistry. It was said to be easy and I found it to be so.

With my preparation for another trial, I made an effort to simplify my life still further. I felt that my way of living was still beyond the modest means of my family. The thought of

IN ENGLAND AS A STUDENT

my struggling brother, who nobly responded to my regular calls for monetary help, deeply pained me. I saw that most of those who were spending from eight to fifteen pounds monthly had the advantage of scholarships. I had before me examples of much simpler living. I came across a fair number of poor students living more humbly than I. One of them was staying in the slums in a room at two shillings a week and living on two pence worth of cocoa and bread per meal from Lockhart's cheap Cocoa Rooms. It was far from me to think of copying him, but I felt I could surely have one room instead of two and cook some of my meals at home. That would be a saving of four to five pounds each month. I also came across books on simple living. I gave up the suite of rooms and rented one instead, invested in a stove, and began cooking my breakfast at home. The process scarcely took me more than twenty minutes for there was only oatmeal porridge to cook and water to boil for cocoa. I had lunch out, and for dinner bread and cocoa at home. Thus I managed to live on a shilling and three pence a day. This was also a period of intensive study. Plain living saved me plenty of time and I passed my examination.

Let not the reader think that this living made my life by any means a dreary affair. On the contrary the change suited me beautifully. It was also more in keeping with the means of my family. My life was certainly more truthful and my soul knew no bounds of joy.

As soon as, or even before, I made alterations in my expenses and my way of living, I began to make changes in my diet. I stopped taking the sweets and spices I had got from home. The mind having taken a different turn, the fondness for spices wore away, and I now relished the boiled spinach which in Richmond tasted insipid, cooked without spices. Many such experiments taught me that taste depended much on one's attitude of mind rather than on the tongue.

The economic consideration was of course constantly before me. There was in those days a body of opinion which regarded tea and coffee as harmful, and favoured cocoa. And as I was convinced that one should eat only articles that nourished the body, I gave up tea and coffee as a rule and took cocoa instead.

There were many minor experiments going on along with the main one: as for example, giving up starchy foods at one time, living on bread and fruit alone at another, and once living on cheese, milk and eggs. This last experiment is worth noting. It lasted not even a fortnight. The reformer who advocated starchless food had spoken highly of eggs and held that eggs were not meat. It was apparent that there was no injury done to living creatures in taking eggs. So I took eggs in spite of my vow. But the lapse was momentary. I had no business to put a new interpretation on the vow. The interpretation of my mother who administered the vow was there for me. I knew that her definition of meat included eggs. And as soon as I saw the true import of the vow I gave up eggs and the experiment alike.

Full of a new convert's zeal for vegetarianism, I decided to start a vegetarian club in my locality. The club went well for a while, but came to an end in the course of a few months. For I

IN ENGLAND AS A STUDENT

left the locality, according to my custom of moving from place to place periodically. But this brief and modest experience gave me some little training in organizing and conducting institutions.

Shyness My Shield

I was elected to the Executive Committee of the Vegetarian Society, and made it a point to attend every one of its meetings, but I always felt tongue-tied. It was only in South Africa that I got over this shyness, though I never completely overcame it. It was impossible for me to speak without preparation. I hesitated whenever I had to face strange audiences and avoided making a speech whenever I could.

I must say that, beyond occasionally exposing me to laughter, my shyness has been no disadvantage whatever. In fact I can see that, on the contrary, it has been all to my advantage. My hesitancy in speech, which was once an annoyance, is now a pleasure. Its greatest benefit has been that it has formed the habit of restraining my thoughts. A man of few words will rarely be thoughtless in his speech; he will measure every word. My shyness has been in reality my shield. It has allowed me to grow. It has helped me in my discovery of truth.

Acquaintance with Religions

Towards the end of my second year in England I came across two Theosophists, brothers, and both unmarried. They talked to me about the *Gita*. They were reading Sir Edwin Arnold's translation – *The Song Celestial* and they invited me to read the original with them. I felt ashamed, as I had read the divine poem neither in Sanskrit nor in Gujarati. I had to tell them that I had not read the *Gita,* but that I would gladly read it with them, and that though my knowledge of Sanskrit was meagre, still I hoped to be able to understand the original to the extent of telling where the translation failed to bring out the meaning. I began reading the *Gita* with them. The verses in the second chapter

> If one,
> Ponders on subjects of the sense, there springs
> Attraction; from attraction grows desire,
> Desire flames to fierce passion, passion breeds
> Recklessness; then the memory—all betrayed—
> Lets noble purpose go, and saps the mind,
> Till purpose, mind, and man are all undone.

made a deep impression on my mind, and they still ring in my ears. The book struck me as one of priceless worth. The impression has ever since been growing on me with the result that I regard it today as the best book for the knowledge of Truth. It has afforded me invaluable help in my moments of gloom.

The brothers also recommended *The Light of Asia*[4] by Sir Advin Arnold, whom I knew till then as the author only of *The Song Celestial,* and I read it with even greater interest than I did the *Bhagavadgita.* Once I had begun it I could not leave

---

4 Given in the form of a poem the message of Lord Buddha. – Ed.

IN ENGLAND AS A STUDENT

off. I recall having read, at the brothers' instance, Madame Blavatsky's *Key to Theosophy*. This book stimulated in me the desire to read books on Hinduism, and made me give up the idea taught by missionaries that Hinduism was full of superstition.

About the same time I met a good Christian from Manchester in a vegetarian boarding house. He talked to me about Christianity. I narrated to him my Rajkot recollections. He was pained to hear them. He said, 'I am a vegetarian. I do not drink. Many Christians are meat-eaters and drink, no doubt; but neither meat-eating nor drinking is enjoined by Scripture. Do please read the Bible.' I accepted his advice, and he got me a copy. I began reading it, but I could not possibly read through the Old Testament.

But the New Testament produced a different impression, especially the Sermon on the Mount[5] which went straight to my heart. I compared it with the *Gita*. The verses, 'But I say unto you, that ye resist not evil; but whosoever shall smite thee on thy right cheek, turn to him the other also. And if any man take away thy coat let him have thy cloak too,' delighted me beyond measure and put me in mind of Shamal Bhatt's 'For a bowl of water, give a goodly meal' etc. My young mind tried to unify the teaching of the *Gita*, the *Light of Asia* and the Sermon on the Mount. That renunciation was the highest form of religion appealed to me greatly.

---

5   Jesus's teachings delivered on a mountainside. See Matthew, Chapters V to VII.

Beyond this acquaintance with religion I could not go at the moment, as reading for the examination left me scarcely any time for outside subjects. But I thought that I should read more religious books and acquaint myself with all the principal religions.

In India as a Barrister

Back in India

I passed my examinations, was called to the Bar on the 10th of June 1891, and enrolled in the High Court on the 11th. On the 12th I sailed for home.

But notwithstanding my study there was no end to my helplessness and fear. I did not feel myself qualified to practise law. I had read the laws, but not learnt how to practise law. Besides, I had learnt nothing at all of Indian law. I had not the slightest idea of Hindu and Mahomedan Law. I had not even learnt how to draft a plaint, and felt completely helpless. I had serious misgivings as to whether I should be able even to earn a living by the profession.

My elder brother had come to meet me at the dock in Bombay. I was pining to see my mother. My brother had kept me ignorant of her death, which had taken place whilst I was still in England. He did not want to give me the bad news in a foreign land. The news was nonetheless a severe shock to me. My grief was even greater than over my father's death. Most of my cherished hopes were shattered. But I remember that I did not give myself up to any wild expression of grief. I could even check the tears, and took to life just as though nothing had happened.

The storm in my caste over my foreign voyage was still there. It had divided the caste into two camps, one of which immediately re-admitted me, while the other was bent on keeping me out. I never tried to seek admission to the section that had refused it. Nor did I feel even mental resentment against any of the headmen of that section. Some of these regarded me with dislike, but I scrupulously avoided hurting their feelings. I fully respected their regulations. According to these, none of my relations, including my father-in-law and mother-in-law, and even my sister and brother-in-law, could entertain me; and I would not so much as drink water at their houses. They were prepared secretly to lay aside the prohibition, but I did not like to do a thing in secret that I would not do in public.

The result of my scrupulous conduct was that I never had occasion to be troubled by the caste; nay, I have experienced nothing but affection and generosity from the general body of the section that still regards me as outside the caste. They have even helped me in my work, without ever expecting me to do anything for the caste. It is my conviction that all these good things are due to my non-resistance. Had I agitated for being admitted to the caste, had I attempted to divide it into more camps, had I provoked the castemen, they would surely have retaliated and I would have found myself in a whirlpool of agitation.

To start practice in Rajkot would have meant sure ridicule. I had hardly the knowledge of a qualified *vakil* and yet I expected to be paid ten times his fee! No client would be fool enough to engage me.

Friends advised me to go to Bombay for some time in order to gain experience of the High Court, to study Indian law and to try and get what cases I could. I took up the suggestion and went. But it was impossible for me to get along in Bombay for more than four or five months, there being no income to square with the ever-increasing expenditure. About this time, I took up the case of one Mamibai. It was a 'small cause'. 'You will have to pay some commission to the tout,'[6] I was told. I emphatically declined. I gave no commission but got Mamibai's case all the same. It was an easy case. I charged Rs 30 for my fees. The case was not likely to last longer than a day.

This was my first appearance in the Small Cause Court. I had to cross-examine the plaintiff's witness. I stood up, but my courage failed. My head was reeling and I felt as though the whole Court was doing likewise. I could think of no question to ask. The judge must have laughed, and the *vakils* no doubt enjoyed the sight. But I could not see anything. I sat down and told the agent that I could not conduct the case, that he had better engage Shri Patel and have the fee back from me.

---

6   A man who obtains cases for lawyers. – Ed

Shri Patel was duly engaged for Rs 51. To him, of course, the case was child's play.

I hastened from the Court, not knowing whether my client won or lost her case, but I was ashamed of myself, and decided not to take up any more cases until I had courage enough to conduct them. So I thought I might take up a teacher's job. My knowledge of English was good enough and I should have loved to teach English to Matriculation boys in some school. In this way I could have met at least part of the expenses. I came across an advertisement in the papers: 'Wanted an English teacher to teach one hour daily. Salary Rs 75.' The advertisement was from a famous high school. I applied for the post and was called for an interview. I went there in high hopes, but when the principal found that I was not a graduate, he regretfully refused me.

'But I have passed the London Matriculation with Latin as my second language.'

'True, but we want a graduate.'

It could not be helped. I was very disappointed. My brother also felt very worried. We both came to the conclusion that it was no use spending more time in Bombay.

So I left Bombay and went to Rajkot, where I set up my own office. Here I got along moderately well. Drafting applications and memorials brought me, on an average, Rs 300 a month. For this work I had to thank influence rather than my own ability, for my brother's partner had a settled practice. All applications etc. which were, really or to his mind, of an important character, he sent to big barristers.

To my lot fell the applications to be drafted on behalf of his poor clients.

The First Shock

My brother had been secretary and adviser to the late Ranasaheb of Porbandar before he was installed on his *gadi,* and my brother at this time suffered under the charge of having given wrong advice when in that office. The matter had gone to the Political Agent who was prejudiced against my brother. Now I had known this officer when in England, and he may be said to have been fairly friendly to me. My brother thought that I should avail myself of the friendship and putting in a good word on his behalf, try to remove the prejudice of the Political Agent. I did not at all like this idea. I should not, I thought, try to take advantage of a trifling acquaintance in England. If my brother was really at fault, what use was my recommendation? If he was innocent, he should submit a petition in the proper course and, confident of his innocence, face the result. My brother did not like this advice. 'You do not know Kathiawad,' he said, 'and you have yet to know the world. Only influence counts here. It is not proper for you, a brother, to shirk your duty, when you can clearly put in a good word about me to an officer you know.'

I could not refuse him, so I went to the officer much against my will. I knew I had no right to approach him and was fully conscious that I was compromising my self-respect. But I sought an appointment and got it. I reminded him of the old acquaintance, but I immediately saw that Kathiawad was different from England; that an officer on leave was not the same as an officer on duty. The Political Agent owned the acquaintance, but the reminder seemed to stiffen him. 'Surely you have not come here to abuse that acquaintance, have you?' appeared to be the meaning of that stiffness, and seemed to be written on his brow. Nevertheless I opened my case. The sahib was impatient. 'Your brother is an intriguer. I want to hear nothing more from you. I have no time. If your brother has anything to say, let him apply through the proper channel.' The answer was enough, was perhaps deserved. But selfishness is blind. I went on with my story. The sahib got up and said: "You must go now.'

'But please hear me out,' said I. That made him more angry. He called his peon and ordered him to show me the door. I was still hesitating when the peon came in, placed his hands on my shoulders and put me out of the room.

The sahib went away, as also the peon, and I departed fretting and fuming. I at once wrote out and sent over a note to this effect: 'You have insulted me. You have assaulted me through your peon. If you make no amends, I shall have to proceed against you.'

Quick came the answer through his *sowar*:

'You were rude to me. I asked you to go and you would not. I had no option but to order my peon to show you the door. Even after he asked you to leave the office, you did not do so. He therefore had to use just enough force to send you out. You are at liberty to proceed as you wish.'

With this answer in my pocket, I came home feeling ashamed, and told my brother all that had happened. He was grieved, but did not know how to console me. He spoke to his *vakil* friends to find out how to proceed against the sahib. Sir Pherozeshah Mehta happened to be in Rajkot at this time, having come down from Bombay for some case. But how could a junior barrister like me dare to see him? So I sent him the papers of my case, through the *vakil* who had engaged him and begged for his advice. 'Tell Gandhi,' he said, 'such things are the common experience of many *vakils* and barristers. He is still fresh from England, and hot-blooded. He does not know British officers. If he would earn something and have an easy time here, let him tear up the note and pocket the insult. He will gain nothing by proceeding against the sahib, and on the contrary will very likely ruin himself. Tell him he has yet to know life.'

The advice was as bitter as poison to me, but I had to swallow it. I pocketed the insult, but also profited by it. 'Never again shall I place myself in such a false position, never again shall I try to exploit friendship in this way,' said I to myself, and since then I have never been guilty of a breach of that determination. This shock changed the course of my life.

I was no doubt at fault in having gone to that officer. But his impatience and overbearing anger were out of all proportion to my mistake. It did not justify expulsion. Now most of my work would naturally be in his court. I had no desire to seek his favour. Indeed, having once threatened to proceed against him, I did not like to remain silent.

Meanwhile, I began to learn something of the petty politics of the country. Kathiawad, being a group of small states, naturally had its rich crop of petty intrigues. Princes were always at the mercy of others and ready to lend their ears to flatterers. Even the sahib's peon had to be coaxed, and the sahib's *shirastedar* was more than his master, as he was his eyes, his ears and his interpreter. The *shirastedar*'s will was law, and his income was always reputed to be more than the sahib's. This may have been an exaggeration, but he certainly lived beyond his salary.

This atmosphere appeared to me to be poisonous, and how to remain in it was a problem for me.

I was thoroughly depressed and my brother clearly saw it. We both felt that, if I could secure some job, I should be free from this atmosphere of intrigue. But without intrigue a ministership or judgeship was out of the question. And the quarrel with the sahib stood in the way of my practice. I did not know what to do.

In the meantime, a Meman firm from Porbandar wrote to my brother making the following offer: 'We have business in South Africa. Ours is a big firm, and we have a big case there in the Court, our claim being £40,000. It has been going on for a long time. We have engaged the services of the best *vakils* and barristers. If you sent your brother there, he would be useful to us and also to himself. He would be able to instruct our lawyer better than ourselves. And he would have the advantage of seeing a new part of the world and of making new acquaintances.'

'How long do you require my services?' I asked. 'And what will be the payment?'

'Not more than a year. We will pay you a first-class return fare and a sum of £105, all found.'

This was hardly going there as a barrister. It was going as a servant of the firm. But I wanted somehow to leave India. There was also the tempting opportunity of seeing a new country, and of having new experience. Also I could send £105 to my brother and help in the expenses of the household. I closed with the offer without any bargaining, and got ready to go to South Africa.

In South Africa

Arrival in South Africa

The port of Natal is Durban also known as Port Natal. Abdulla Sheth was there to receive me. As the ship arrived at the quay and I watched the people coming on board to meet their friends, I observed that Indians were not held in much respect. I could not fail to notice a sort of snobbishness about the manner in which those who knew Abdulla Sheth behaved towards him, and it stung me. Abdulla Sheth had got used to it. Those who looked at me did so with a certain amount of curiosity. My dress marked me out from other Indians. I had a frock-coat and a turban, in imitation of the Bengal *pugree*.

On the second or third day after my arrival, he took me to see the Durban court. There he introduced me to several people and seated me next to his attorney. The Magistrate kept staring at me and finally asked me to take off my turban. This I refused to do and left the court.

IN SOUTH AFRICA

So here too there was fighting in store for me.

I wrote to the press about the incident and defended the wearing of my turban in the court. The question was very much discussed in the papers, which described me as an 'unwelcome visitor'. Thus the incident gave me an unexpected advertisement in South Africa within a few days of my arrival there. My turban stayed with me practically until the end of my stay in South Africa.

To Pretoria

The firm received a letter from their lawyers saying preparations should be made for the case, and that Abdulla Sheth should go to Pretoria himself or send a representative. Abdulla Sheth gave me this letter to read, and asked me if I would go to Pretoria. 'I can only say after I have understood the case from you,' said I. 'At present I do not know what I have to do there.' He thereupon asked his clerks to explain the case to me.

On the seventh or eighth day after my arrival, I left Durban. A first-class seat was booked for me. It was usual there to pay five shillings extra, if one needed a bedding. Abdulla Sheth insisted that I should book a bedding, but out of obstinacy and pride and with a view to saving five shillings, I declined. Abdulla Sheth warned me. 'Look, now,' said he, 'this is a different country from India. Thank God, we have enough and to spare. Please do not stint yourself in anything that you may need.'

I thanked him and asked him not to be anxious.

The train reached Maritzburg, the capital of Natal, at about 9 p.m. Beddings used to be provided at this station.

A railway servant came and asked me if I wanted one. 'No,' said I, 'I have one with me.' He went away. But a passenger came next, and looked me up and down. He saw that I was a 'coloured' man. This disturbed him. Out he went and came in again with one or two officials. They all kept quiet, when another official came to me and said, 'Come along, you must go to the van compartment.'

'But I have a first-class ticket,' said I.

'That doesn't matter,' rejoined the other. 'I tell you, you must go to the van compartment.'

'I tell you, I was permitted to travel in this compartment at Durban, and I insist on going on in it.'

'No, you won't,' said the official. 'You must leave this compartment, or else I shall have to call a police constable to push you out.'

'Yes, you may. I refuse to get out voluntarily.'

The constable came. He took me by the hand and pushed me out. My luggage was also taken out. I refused to go to the other compartment and the train steamed away. I went and sat in the waiting room, keeping my handbag with me, and leaving the other luggage where it was. The railway authorities had taken charge of it.

It was winter, and winter in the higher regions of South Africa is severely cold. Maritzburg being at a high altitude, the cold was extremely bitter. My overcoat was in my luggage, but I did not dare to ask for it lest I should be insulted again, so I sat and shivered. There was no light in the room. A passenger came in at about midnight and possibly wanted to talk to me. But I was in no mood to talk.

I began to think of my duty. Should I fight for my rights or go back to India, or should I go on to Pretoria without minding the insults, and return to India after finishing the case? It would be cowardice to run back to India without fulfilling my obligation. The hardship to which I was subjected was superficial – only a symptom of the deep disease of colour prejudice. I should try, if possible, to root out the disease and suffer hardships in the process. Redress for wrongs I should seek only to the extent that would be necessary for the removal of the colour prejudice.

So, I decided to take the next available train to Pretoria.

The following morning I sent a long telegram to the General Manager of the Railway and also informed Abdulla Sheth, who immediately met the General Manager. The Manager justified the conduct of the railway authorities, but informed him that he had already instructed the Station Master to see that I reached my destination. Abdulla Sheth wired to the Indian merchants in Maritzburg and to friends in other places to meet me and look after me. The merchants came to see me at the station and tried to comfort me by narrating their own hardships and explaining that what had happened to me was nothing unusual. They also said that Indians travelling first or second class had to expect trouble from railway officials and white passengers. The day was thus spent in listening to these tales of woe. The evening train arrived. There was a reserved berth for me. I now purchased at Maritzburg the bedding ticket I had refused to book at Durban.

The train reached Charlestown in the morning. There was no railway, in those days, between Charlestown and

Johannesburg, but only a stage-coach, which halted at Standerton for the night *en route*. I possessed a ticket for the coach, which was not cancelled by the break of journey at Maritzburg for a day; besides, Abdulla Sheth had sent a wire to the coach agent at Charlestown.

But the agent only needed a pretext for putting me off, and so, when he discovered me to be a stranger, he said, 'Your ticket is cancelled.' I gave him the proper reply. The reason at the back of his mind was not want of accommodation, but quite another. Passengers had to be accommodated inside the coach, but as I was regarded as a 'coolie' and looked a stranger, it would be proper, thought the 'leader', as the white man in charge of the coach was called, not to seat me with the white passengers. There were seats on either side of the coachbox. The leader sat on one of these as a rule. Today he sat inside and gave me his seat. I knew it was sheer injustice and an insult, but I thought it better to pocket it. I could not have forced myself inside, and if I had raised a protest, the coach would have gone off without me. This would have meant the loss of another day, and Heaven only knows what would have happened the next day. So, much as I fretted within myself, I prudently sat next to the coachman.

At about three o'clock the coach reached Pardekoph. Now the leader desired to sit where I was seated, as he wanted to smoke and possibly to have some fresh air. So he took a piece of dirty sack-cloth from the driver, spread it on the footboard and, addressing me said, 'Sami, you sit on this, I want to sit near the driver.' The insult was more than I could bear. In fear and trembling I said to him, 'It was you who seated me here, though I should have been accommodated inside. I put up with the insult. Now that you want to sit outside and smoke, you would have me sit at your feet. I will not do so, but I am prepared to sit inside.'

As I was struggling through these sentences, the man came down upon me and began heavily to box my ears. He seized me by the arm and tried to drag me down. I clung to the brass rails of the coachbox and was determined to keep my hold even at the risk of breaking my wristbones. The passengers were witnessing the scene – the man swearing at me, dragging and beating me, and I remaining still. He was strong, and I was weak. Some of the passengers were moved to pity and exclaimed: 'Man, let him alone. Don't beat him. He is not to blame. He is right. If he can't stay there, let him come and sit with us.' 'No fear,' cried the man, but he seemed somewhat ashamed and stopped beating me. He let go my arm, swore at me a little more, and asking the Hottentot servant who was sitting on the other side of the coachbox to sit on the footboard, took the seat so vacated.

The passengers took their seats and, the whistle given, the coach rattled away. My heart was beating fast within my breast, and I was wondering whether I should ever reach my destination alive. The man cast an angry look at me now and then and, pointing his finger at me, growled: 'Take care, let me once get to Standerton and I shall show you what I can do.' I sat speechless and prayed to God to help me.

After dark we reached Standerton and I heaved a sigh of relief on seeing some Indian faces. As soon as I got down, these friends said: 'We are here to receive you and take you to

Isa Sheth's shop. We have had a telegram from Dada Abdulla.'
I was very glad, and we went to Sheth Isa Haji Summar's shop.

I wanted to inform the agent of the Coach Company of the whole affair. So I wrote him a letter, narrating everything that had happened, and drawing his attention to the threat this man had held out. I also asked for an assurance that he would accommodate me with the other passengers inside the coach when we started the next morning. To which the agent replied to this effect: 'From Standerton we have a bigger coach with different men in charge. The man complained of will not be there tomorrow, and you will have a seat with the other passengers.' This somewhat relieved me. I had, of course, no intention of proceeding against the man who had assaulted me, and so the chapter of the assault closed there.

In the morning Isa Sheth's man took me to the coach. I got a good seat and reached Johannesburg quite safely that night.

Standerton is a small village and Johannesburg a big city. Abdulla Sheth had wired to Johannesburg also and given me the name and address of Muhammad Kasam Kamruddin's firm there. Their man had come to receive me at the stage, but neither did I see him nor did he recognize me. So I decided to go to a hotel. I knew the names of several. Taking a cab I asked to be driven to the Grand National Hotel. I saw the Manager and asked for a room. He looked at me for a moment, and politely saying, 'I am very sorry, we are full up,' bade me goodbye. So I asked the cabman to drive to Muhammad Kasam Kamruddin's shop. Here I found Abdul Gani Sheth expecting me, and he gave me a cordial greeting. He had a hearty laugh over the story of my experience at the hotel. 'However did you expect to be admitted to a hotel?' he said.

'Why not?' I asked.

'You will come to know after you have stayed here a few days,' said he.

'Look now, you have to go to Pretoria tomorrow. You will have to travel third class. Conditions in the Transvaal are worse than in Natal. First and second class tickets are never issued to Indians.'

I sent for the railway regulations and read them. There was a loophole. The language of the old Transvaal enactments was not very exact or precise; that of the railway regulations was even less so.

I said to the Sheth: 'I wish to go first class, and if I cannot, I shall prefer to take a cab to Pretoria, a matter of only thirty-seven miles.'

Sheth Abdul Gani drew my attention to the extra time and money this would mean, but agreed to my proposal to travel first, and accordingly we sent a note to the station master. I mentioned in my note that I was a barrister and that I always travelled first. I also stated in the letter that I needed to reach Pretoria as early as possible, that as there was no time to await his reply I would receive it in person at the station, and that I should expect to get a first-class ticket. There was of course a purpose behind asking for the reply in person. I thought that, if the station master gave a written reply, he would certainly say 'no', especially because he would have his own notion of a 'coolie' barrister. I would therefore appear before him in faultless English dress, talk to him and possibly persuade him to issue a first class ticket. So I went to the station master in a frock-coat and necktie, placed a sovereign for my fare on the counter and asked for a first-class ticket.

'You sent me that note?' he asked.

'That is so. I shall be much obliged if you will give me a ticket. I must reach Pretoria today.'

He smiled and, moved to pity, said: 'I am not a Transvaaler. I am a Hollander. I appreciate your feelings, and you have my sympathy. I do want to give you a ticket – on one condition, however, that, if the guard should ask you to shift to the third class, you will not involve me in the affair, by which I mean that you should not proceed against the railway company. I wish you a safe journey. I can see you are a gentleman.'

With these words he booked the ticket. I thanked him and gave him the necessary assurance.

Sheth Abdul Gani had come to see me off at the station. The incident gave him an agreeable surprise, but he warned me saying: 'I shall be thankful if you reach Pretoria all right. I am afraid the guard will not leave you in peace in the first class and even if he does, the passengers will not.'

I took my seat in a first-class compartment and the train started. At Germiston the guard came to examine the tickets. He was angry to find me there, and signalled to me with his finger to go to the third class. I showed him my first-class ticket. 'That does not matter,' said he, 'remove to the third class.' There was only one English passenger in the compartment. He took the guard to task. 'What do you mean by troubling the gentleman?' he said. 'Don't you see he has a first-class ticket? I do not mind in the least his travelling with me.' Addressing me, he said, 'You should make yourself comfortable where you are.' The guard muttered: 'If you want to travel with a coolie, what do I care?' and went away.

At about eight o'clock in the evening the train reached Pretoria.

First Day in Pretoria

Pretoria station in 1893 was quite different from what it was in 1914. The lights were burning dimly. The travellers were few. I let all the other passengers go and thought that, as soon as the ticket collector was fairly free, I would hand him my ticket and ask him if he could direct me to some small hotel or any other such place where I might go; otherwise I would spend the night at the station. I must confess I shrank from asking him even this, for I was afraid of being insulted.

The station became clear of all passengers. I gave my ticket to the ticket collector and began my inquiries. He replied to me courteously, but I saw that he could not be of any considerable help. But an American Negro who was standing nearby broke into the conversation.

'I see,' said he, 'that you are an utter stranger here, without any friends. If you will come with me I will take you to a small hotel, of which the proprietor is an American who is very well known to me. I think he will accept you.'

I had my own doubts about the offer, but I thanked him and accepted his suggestion. He took me to Johnston's Family Hotel. He drew Mr Johnston aside to speak to him, and the latter agreed to accommodate me for the night, on condition that I should have my dinner served in my room.

'I assure you,' said he, 'that I have no colour prejudice. But I have only European custom, and, if I allowed you to eat in the dining room, my guests might be offended and even go away.'

'Thank you,' said I, 'even for accommodating me for the night. I am now more or less acquainted with the conditions here, and I understand your difficulty. I do not mind your serving the dinner in my room. I hope to be able to make some other arrangement tomorrow.'

I was shown into a room where I now sat waiting for the dinner and thinking, as I was quite alone. There were not many guests in the hotel, and I had expected the waiter to come very shortly with the dinner. Instead Mr Johnston appeared. He said: 'I was ashamed of having asked you to have your dinner here. So I spoke to the other guests about you, and asked them if they would mind your having your dinner in the dining room. They said they had no objection, and that they did not mind your staying here as long as you liked. Please, therefore, come to the dining room, if you will, and stay here as long as you wish.' I thanked him again, went to the dining room and had a hearty dinner.

Next morning I called on the attorney, Mr A.W. Baker. Abdulla Sheth had given me some description of him, so his cordial reception did not surprise me. He received me very warmly and made kind inquiries. I explained all about myself. Thereupon he said: 'We have no work for you here as barrister, for we have engaged the best lawyer. The case is a prolonged and complicated one, so I shall take your assistance only to the extent of getting necessary information. And of course, you will make communication with my client easy for me, as I shall now ask for all the information I want from him through you. That is certainly an advantage. I have not yet found rooms for you. I thought I had better do so after having seen you. There is a fearful amount of colour prejudice here, and therefore it is not easy to find lodging for such as you. But I know a poor woman. She is the wife of a baker. I think she will take you and thus add to her income at the same time. Come, let us go to her place.'

So he took me to her house. He spoke with her privately about me, and she agreed to accept me as a boarder at 35 shillings a week.

Getting Acquainted with the Indian Problem

My stay in Pretoria enabled me to make a deep study of the social, economic and political condition of the Indians in the Transvaal and the Orange Free State. I had no idea that this study was to be of invaluable service to me in the future.

It was provided under the amended law that all Indians should pay a poll tax of £3 as fee for entry into the Transvaal. They might not own land except in places set apart for them, and in practice even that was not to be ownership. They had no vote. All this was under the special law for Asiatics, to whom the laws for the coloured people were also applied.

Under the latter, Indians might not walk on public footpaths, and might not move out of doors after 9 p.m. without a permit. I often went out at night for a walk with a friend, Mr Coates, and we rarely got back home much before ten o'clock. What if the police arrested me? Mr Coates was more concerned about this than I. He had to issue passes to his Negro servants. But how could he give one to me? Only a master might issue a permit to a servant. If I had wanted one, and even if Mr Coates had been ready to give it, he could not have done so, for it would have been fraud.

So Mr Coates or some friend of his took me to the State Attorney, Dr Krause. We turned out to be barristers of the same Inn. The fact that I needed a pass to enable me to be out of doors after 9 p.m. was too much for him. He expressed sympathy for me. Instead of ordering for me a pass, he gave me a letter authorizing me to be out of doors at all hours without police interference. I always kept this letter on me whenever I went out. The fact that I never had to make use of it was a mere accident.

The consequences of the regulation regarding the use of footpaths were rather serious for me. I always went out for a walk through President Street to an open plain. President Kruger's house was in this street – a very modest building without a garden and, not distinguishable from other houses in its neighbourhood.

Only the presence of a policeman before the house indicated that it belonged to some official. I nearly always went along the footpath past this patrol without the slightest hitch or hindrance.

Now the man on duty used to be changed from time to time. Once one of these men, without giving me the slightest warning, without even asking me to leave the footpath, pushed and kicked me onto the street. I was dismayed. Before I could question him about his behaviour, Mr Coates, who happened to be passing the spot on horseback, hailed me and said:

'Gandhi, I have seen everything. I shall gladly be your witness in court if you proceed against the man. I am very sorry you have been so rudely assaulted.'

'You need not be sorry,' I said. 'What does the poor man know? All coloured people are the same to him. He no doubt treats Negroes just as he has treated me. I have made it a rule not to go to court in respect of any personal grievance. So I do not intend to proceed against him.'

'That is just like you,' said Mr Coates, 'but do think it over again. We must teach such men a lesson.' He then spoke to the policeman and scolded him. I could not follow their talk as it was in Dutch, the policeman being a Boer. But he apologized to me, for which there was no need. I had already forgiven him.

But I never again went through this street. There would be other men coming in this man's place and ignorant of the incident, they would behave likewise. Why should I unnecessarily court another kick? I therefore selected a different walk.

I saw that South Africa was no country for a self-respecting Indian, and my mind became more and more occupied with the question as to how this state of things might be improved. But my principal duty for the moment was to attend to the case of Dada Abdulla.

The Case

I saw that the facts of Dada Abdulla's case made it very strong indeed, and that the law was bound to be on his side. But I also saw that the case, if it were persisted in, would ruin both him and his opponent, who were relatives and both belonged to the same city. No one knew how long the case might go on. I felt that my duty was to befriend both parties and bring them together. I strained every nerve to bring about a compromise and succeeded.

Both were happy over the result, and both rose in the public estimation. My joy was boundless. I had learnt the true practice of law. I had learnt to find out the better side of human nature and to enter men's hearts. I realized that the true function of a lawyer was to unite parties driven apart by a quarrel. The lesson was so burnt into me that a large part of my time during the twenty years of my practice as a lawyer was occupied in bringing about private compromises of hundreds of cases. I lost nothing thereby – not even money, certainly not my soul.

Man Proposes, God Disposes

The case having been concluded, I had no reason for staying in Pretoria. So I went back to Durban and began to make preparations for my return home. But Abdulla Sheth was not the man to let me sail without a send-off. He gave a farewell party in my honour at Sydenham.

It was proposed to spend the whole day there. Whilst I was turning over the sheets of some of the newspapers I found there, I chanced to see a paragraph in a corner of one of them under the title 'Indian Franchise'. It was with reference to the Bill then before the House of Legislature, which sought to deprive the Indians of their right to elect members of the

Natal Legislative Assembly. I was ignorant of the Bill and so were the rest of the guests who had gathered there.

I inquired of Abdulla Sheth about it. He said: 'What can we understand in these matters? We can only understand things that affect our trade.' But I was on the point of returning home and hesitated to express what was passing through my mind in this matter. I simply said to Abdulla Sheth: 'This Bill, if it passes into law, will make our lot extremely difficult. It strikes at the root of our self-respect.'

The other guests were listening to this conversation with attention. One of them said: 'Shall I tell you what should be done? You cancel your passage by this boat, stay here a month longer, and we will fight as you direct us.' All the others supported him.

It was now impossible for me to leave Natal. The Indian friends surrounded me on all sides and begged me to remain there permanently. Thus I settled in Natal. Continued agitation was essential for making an impression on the Secretary of State for the Colonies. For this purpose it was thought necessary to bring into being a permanent organization. So I consulted Sheth Abdulla and other friends, and we all decided to have a public organization of a permanent character, and on the 22nd May the Natal Indian Congress came into being.

The £3 Tax

About the year 1860 the Europeans in Natal, finding that there was considerable scope for sugarcane cultivation, felt themselves in need of labour. Without outside labour the cultivation of cane and the manufacture of sugar were impossible, as the Natal Zulus were not suited to this form of work. The Natal Government therefore corresponded with the Indian Government, and secured their permission to recruit Indian labour. These recruits were to sign an agreement or indenture to work in Natal for five years, and at the end of the term they were to be at liberty to settle there and to have full rights of ownership of land. Those were the inducements held out to them.

But the Indians gave more than had been expected of them. They grew large quantities of vegetables. They introduced a number of Indian varieties and made it possible to grow the local varieties cheaper. They also introduced the mango. Nor did their enterprise stop at agriculture. They entered trade. They purchased land for building, and many raised themselves from the status of labourers to that of owners of land and houses. Merchants from India followed them and settled there for trade.

The white traders were alarmed. When they first welcomed the Indian labourers, they did not know their business skill. They might be tolerated as independent agriculturists, but their competition in trade could not be allowed.

This sowed the seed of the antagonism to Indians. Many other factors contributed to its growth. Through legislation this antagonism found its expression in a bill to impose a tax on the indentured Indians.

We organized a fierce campaign against this tax. Had the community given up the struggle, had the Congress abandoned the campaign and submitted to the tax as inevitable, the hated tax would have continued to be levied from the indentured

IN SOUTH AFRICA

Indians until this day, to the eternal shame of the Indians in South Africa and of the whole of India.

By now I had been three years in South Africa. I had got to know the people and they had got to know me. In 1896 I asked permission to go home for six months, for I saw that I was in for a long stay there. I had established a fairly good practice, and could see that people felt the need of my presence. So I made up my mind to go home, fetch my wife and children, and then return and settle out there. I also saw that, if I went home, I might be able to do there some public work by educating public opinion and creating more interest in the Indians in South Africa.

Visit to India

In India

I went straight to Rajkot without halting at Bombay and began to make preparations for writing a pamphlet on the situation in South Africa. The writing and publication of the pamphlet took about a month. It had a green cover and came to be known afterwards as the Green Pamphlet. In it I drew a purposely subdued picture of the condition of Indians in South Africa. Ten thousand copies were printed and sent to all the papers and leaders of every party in India. A summary of the article was cabled by Reuter to England, and a summary of that summary was cabled to Natal by Reuter's London office. This cable was not longer than three lines in print. It was a brief, but exaggerated, edition of the picture I had drawn of the treatment accorded to the Indians in Natal, and it was not in my words. We shall see later on the effect this had in Natal.

VISIT TO INDIA

In the meanwhile, every paper of note commented at length on the question.

To get these pamphlets ready for posting was no small matter. It would have been expensive too, if I had employed paid help for preparing wrappers etc. But I hit upon a much simpler plan. I gathered together all the children in my locality and asked them to volunteer two or three hours' labour of a morning, when they had no school. This they willingly agreed to do. I promised to bless them, and give them, as a reward, used postage stamps which I had collected. They got through the work in no time. That was my first experiment of having little children as volunteers. Two of those little friends are my co-workers today.

It was my intention to educate public opinion in cities on this question by organizing meetings, and Bombay was the first city I chose. After Bombay and Poona I went to Madras, and from Madras I proceeded to Calcutta. There I received the following cable from Durban: 'Parliament opens January. Return soon.'

So in the beginning of December, I set sail second time for South Africa, now with my wife and two sons and the only son of my widowed sister. Another steamship *Naderi* also sailed for Durban at the same time. The agents of the Company were Dada Abdulla and Co. The total number of passengers these boats carried must have been about eight hundred, half of whom were bound for the Transvaal.

Back in South Africa

Stormy Arrival in South Africa

The two ships cast anchor in the port of Durban on or about the 18th of December. No passengers are allowed to land at any of the South African ports before being subjected to a thorough medical examination. If the ship has any passenger suffering from contagious disease, she has to undergo a period of quarantine. As there had been plague in Bombay when we set sail, we feared that we might have to go through a brief quarantine. The doctor came and examined us. He ordered a five days' quarantine because, in his opinion, plague germs took twenty-three days at the most to develop. Our ship was therefore ordered to be put in quarantine until the twenty-third day of our sailing from Bombay. But this quarantine order had more than health reasons behind it.

The white residents of Durban had been agitating for our repatriation, and the agitation was one of the reasons for the order. Dada Abdulla and Co. kept us regularly informed about the daily happenings in the town. The whites were holding monster meetings every day. On one side there was a handful of poor Indians and a few of their English friends, and on the other were ranged the white men, strong in arms, in numbers, in education and in wealth. They had also the backing of the State, for the Natal Government openly helped them.

We arranged all sorts of games on the ships for the entertainment of the passengers. I took part in the merriment, but my heart was in the combat that was going on in Durban. For I was the real target. There were two charges against me:

1. that whilst in India I had indulged in unmerited condemnation of the Natal whites;
2. that with a view to swamping Natal with Indians I had specially brought the two shiploads of passengers to settle there.

But I was absolutely innocent. I had induced no one to go to Natal. I did not know the passengers when they embarked. And with the exception of a couple of relatives, I did not know the name and address of even one of the hundreds of passengers on board. Neither had I said, whilst in India, a word about the whites in Natal that I had not already said in Natal itself. And I had ample evidence in support of all that I had said.

Thus the days dragged on their weary length.

At the end of twenty-three days the ships were permitted to enter the harbour, and orders permitting the passengers to land were passed.

So the ships were brought into the dock and the passengers began to go ashore. But Mr Escombe, a member of the Cabinet, had sent word to the captain that, as the whites were highly enraged against me and my life was in danger, my family and I should be advised to land at dusk, when the Port Superintendent, Mr Tatum, would escort us home. The captain communicated the message to me, and I agreed to act accordingly. But scarcely half an hour after this, Mr Laughton, a friend and advocate of the Indian community in Durban, came to the captain. He said: 'I would like to take Mr Gandhi with me, should he have no objection. As the legal adviser of the Agent Company I tell you that you are not bound to carry out the message you have received from Mr Escombe.' After this he came to me and said somewhat to this effect: 'If you are not afraid, I suggest that Mrs Gandhi and the children should drive to Mr Rustomji's house, whilst you and I follow them on foot. I do not at all like the idea of your entering the city like a thief in the night. I do not think there is any fear of anyone hurting you. Everything is quiet now. The whites have all dispersed. But in any case I am convinced that you ought not to enter the city stealthily.' I readily agreed. My wife and children drove safely to Mr Rustomji's place. With the captain's permission I went ashore with Mr Laughton. Mr Rustomji's house was about two miles from the dock.

As soon as we landed, some youngsters recognized me and shouted 'Gandhi, Gandhi.' About half a dozen men rushed to the spot and joined in the shouting. Mr Laughton feared that the crowd might swell and hailed a rickshaw. I had never liked the idea of being in a rickshaw. This was to be my first experience. But the youngsters would not let me get into it. They frightened the rickshaw boy out of his life, and he took to his heels. As we went ahead the crowd continued to swell, until it became impossible to proceed further. They first caught hold of Mr Laughton and separated us. Then they pelted me with stones, brickbats and rotten eggs. Someone snatched away my turban, whilst others began to beat and kick me. I fainted and caught hold of the front railings of a house and stood there to get my breath. But it was impossible. They came upon me boxing and beating. The wife of the Police Superintendent, who knew me, happened to be passing by. The brave lady came up, opened her umbrella though there was no sun then, and stood between the crowd and me. This checked the fury of the mob, as it was difficult for them to deliver blows on me without harming Mrs Alexander.

Meanwhile, an Indian youth who witnessed the incident had run to the police station. The Police Superintendent, Mr Alexander, sent a few men to ring me round and take me safely to my destination. They arrived in time. The police station lay on our way. As we reached there, the Superintendent asked me to take refuge in the station, but I gratefully declined the offer. 'They are sure to quieten down when they realize their mistake,' I said. 'I have trust in their sense of fairness.' Escorted by the police, I arrived without further harm at Mr Rustomji's place. I had bruises all over, but no wounds except in one place. Dr Dadibarjor, the ship's doctor, who was on the spot, rendered the best possible help.

There was quiet inside, but outside the whites surrounded the house. Night was coming on, and the yelling crowd was shouting, 'We must have Gandhi.' The quick-sighted Police Superintendent was already there trying to keep the crowds under control, not by threats, but by humouring them. But he was not entirely free from anxiety. He sent me a message to this effect: 'If you would save your friend's house and property and also your family, you should escape from the house in disguise, as I suggest.'

As suggested by the Superintendent, I put on an Indian constable's uniform and wore on my head a Madrasi scarf, wrapped round a plate to serve as a helmet. Two detectives accompanied me, one of them disguised as an Indian merchant and with his face painted to resemble that of an Indian. I forget the disguise of the other. We reached a neighbouring shop by a by-lane and, making our way through the gunny bags piled in the godown, escaped by the gate of the shop and made our way through the crowd to a carriage that had been kept for me at the end of the street. In this we drove off to the same police station where Mr Alexander had offered me refuge a short time before, and I thanked him and the detective officers.

Whilst I had been thus effecting my escape, Mr Alexander had kept the crowd amused by singing the tune:

'Hang old Gandhi!
On the sour apple tree.'

When he was informed of my safe arrival at the police station, he thus broke the news to the crowd: 'Well, your victim has made good his escape through a neighbouring shop. You had better go home now.' Some of them were angry, others laughed, some refused to believe the story.

'Well then,' said the Superintendent, 'if you do not believe me, you may appoint one or two representatives, whom I am ready to take inside the house. If they succeed in finding out Gandhi, I will gladly deliver him to you. But if they fail, you must disperse. I am sure that you have no intention of destroying Mr Rustomji's house or of harming Mr Gandhi's wife and children.'

The crowd sent their representatives to search the house. They soon returned with disappointing news, and the crowd broke up at last, most of them admiring the Superintendent's tactful handling of the situation, and a few fretting and fuming.

The late Mr Chamberlain, who was then Secretary of State for the Colonies, cabled asking the Natal Government to prosecute my assailants. Mr Escombe sent for me, expressed his regret for the injuries I had sustained, and said: 'Believe me, I cannot feel happy over the least little injury done to your person. You had a right to accept Mr Laughton's advice and to face the worst, but I am sure that, if you had considered my suggestion favourably, these sad occurrences would not have happened. If you can identify the assailants, I am prepared to arrest and prosecute them. Mr Chamberlain also desires me to do so.'

To which I gave the following reply:

'I do not want to prosecute anyone. It is possible that I may be able to identify one or two of them, but what is the use of getting them punished? Besides, I do not hold the assailants to blame. They were given to understand that I had made exaggerated and damaging statements in India about the whites in Natal. If they believed these reports, it is no wonder that they were enraged. The leaders and, if you will permit me to say so, you are to blame. You could have guided the people properly, but you also believed Reuter and assumed that I must have indulged in exaggeration. I do not want to prosecute anyone. I am sure that, when the truth becomes known, they will be sorry for their conduct.'

'Would you mind giving me this in writing?' said Mr Escombe. 'Because I shall have to cable to Mr Chamberlain to that effect. I do not want you to make any statement in haste. You may, if you like, consult Mr Laughton and your other friends, before you come to a final decision. I may confess, however, that, if you set aside the right of prosecuting your assailants, you will considerably help me in restoring quiet, besides increasing your own reputation.'

'Thank you,' said I. 'I need not consult anyone. I had made my decision in the matter before I came to you. It is my conviction that I should not prosecute the assailants, and I am prepared this moment to reduce my decision to writing.'

With this I gave him the necessary statement.

On the day of landing, a representation of the *Natal Advertiser* had come to interview me. He had asked me a number of questions, and in reply I had been able to refute every one of the charges that had been levelled against me.

This interview and my refusal to prosecute the assailants produced such a profound impression that the Europeans of Durban were ashamed of their conduct. The press declared me to be innocent and condemned the mob. Thus the lynching ultimately proved to be a blessing for me, that is, for the cause. It increased the prestige of the Indian community in South Africa and made my work easier. In three or four days I went to my house, and it was not long before I settled down again.

Simple Life

The washerman's bill was heavy, and as he was besides by no means noted for his punctuality, even two to three dozen shirts and collars proved insufficient for me. Collars had to be changed daily and shirts, if not daily, at least every alternate day. This meant a double expense, which appeared to me unnecessary. So I equipped myself with a washing outfit to save it. I bought a book on washing, studied the art and taught it also to my wife. This no doubt added to my work, but its novelty made it a pleasure.

I shall never forget the first collar that I washed myself. I had used more starch than necessary, the iron had not been made hot enough, and for fear of burning the collar I had not pressed it sufficiently. The result was that, though the collar was fairly stiff, the superfluous starch continually dropped off it. I went to court with the collar on, thus inviting the ridicule of brother barristers, but even in those days I could be indifferent to ridicule.

'Well,' said I, 'this is my first experience at washing my own collars and hence the loose starch. But it does not trouble me, and then there is the advantage of providing you with so much fun.'

'But surely, there is no lack of laundries here?' asked a friend.

'The laundry bill is very heavy,' said I. 'The charge for washing a collar is almost as much as its price, and even then there is the eternal dependence on the washerman. I prefer by far to wash my things myself.'

In the same way, as I freed myself from slavery to the washerman, I threw off dependence on the barber. All people who go to England learn there at least the art of shaving, but none, to my knowledge, learn to cut their own hair. I had to learn that too. I once went to an English hair-cutter in Pretoria. He contemptuously refused to cut my hair. I certainly felt hurt, but immediately purchased a pair of clippers and cut my hair before the mirror. I succeeded more or less in cutting the front hair, but I spoiled the back. The friends in the court shook with laughter.

'What's wrong with your hair, Gandhi? Rats have been at it?'

'No. The white barber would not condescend to touch my black hair,' said I, 'so I preferred to cut it myself, no matter how badly.'

The reply did not surprise the friends.

The barber was not at fault in having refused to cut my hair. There was every chance of his losing his customers, if he should serve black men. We do not allow our barbers to serve our 'untouchable' brethren. I got the reward of this in South Africa, not once, but many times, and the conviction that it was the punishment for our own sins saved me from becoming angry.

A Recollection and Penance

When I was practising in Durban, my office clerks often stayed with me, and there were among them Hindus and Christians, or to describe them by their provinces, Gujaratis and Tamilians. I do not recollect having ever regarded them as anything but my kith and kin. One of the clerks was a Christian, born of so-called untouchable parents.

The house was built after the Western model and the rooms rightly had no outlets for dirty water. Each room had therefore chamber-pots. Rather than have these cleaned by a servant or, a sweeper, my wife or I attended to them. The clerks who made themselves completely at home would naturally clean their own pots, but the Christian clerk was a newcomer, and it was our duty to attend to his bedroom. My wife managed the pots of the others, but to clean those used by one who had been 'untouchable' seemed to her to be the limit, and we fell out. She could not bear the pots being cleaned by me, neither did she like doing it herself. Even today I can recall the picture of her scolding me, her eyes red with anger and tears streaming down her cheeks, as she descended the staircase, pot in hand. But I was a cruelly kind husband. I regarded myself as her teacher, and so troubled her out of my blind love for her.

I was far from being satisfied by her merely carrying the pot. I would have her do it cheerfully. So I said, raising my voice: 'I will not stand this nonsense in my house.'

The words pierced her like an arrow.

She shouted back: 'Keep your house to yourself and let me go.' I forgot myself, and the spring of compassion dried up in me. I caught her by the hand, dragged the helpless woman to the gate, which was just opposite the staircase, and proceeded to open it with the intention of pushing her out. The tears were running down her cheeks in torrents, and she cried: 'Have you no sense of shame? Must you go so far that you forget yourself? Where am I to go? I have no parents or relatives there to shelter me. Being your wife, you think I must put up with your cuffs and kicks? For heaven's sake, behave yourself, and shut the gate. Let us not be found making scenes like this!'

I put on a brave face, but was really ashamed and shut the gate. If my wife could not leave me, neither could I leave her. We have had numerous quarrels, but the end has always been peace between us. The wife, with her matchless powers of endurance, has always been the victor.

The Boer War

I must skip many other experiences of the period between 1897 and 1899 and come straight to the Boer War.

I have minutely dealt with the inner struggle regarding this in my *History of Satyagraha in South Africa*, and I must not repeat the argument here. I invite the curious to turn to those pages. Suffice it to say that my loyalty to the British rule drove me to participation with the British in that war. I felt that, if I demanded rights as a British citizen, it was also my duty, as such, to participate in the defence of the British Empire.

Our corps was 1,100 strong, with nearly 40 leaders. During these days we had to march for twenty to twenty-five miles a day, bearing the wounded on stretchers. Amongst the wounded we had the honour of carrying soldiers like General Woodgate. The corps was disbanded after six weeks' service.

Our humble work was at the moment much praised, and the Indians' prestige was enhanced.

Costly Gifts

On my relief from war duty I felt that my work was no longer in South Africa but in India. Friends at home were also pressing me to return, and I felt that I should be of more service in India. So I requested my co-workers to relieve me. After very great difficulty my request was conditionally accepted, the condition being that I should be ready to go back to South Africa if, within a year, the community should need me. Farewell meetings were arranged at every place, and costly gifts were presented to me. The gifts of course included things in gold and silver, but there were articles of diamond as well.

The evening I was presented with the bulk of these things I had a sleepless night. I walked up and down my room deeply agitated, but could find no solution. It was difficult for me to forgo gifts worth hundreds, it was more difficult to keep them.

And even if I could keep them, what about my children? What about my wife? They were being trained to a life of service and to an understanding that service was its own reward.

I had no costly ornaments in the house. We had been fast simplifying our life. How then could we afford to have gold watches? How could we afford to wear gold chains and diamond rings? Even then I was telling people to conquer the infatuation for jewellery. What was I now to do with the jewellery that had come upon me?

I decided that I could not keep these things. I drafted a letter, creating a trust of them in favour of the community and appointing Parsi Rustomji and others trustees. In the morning I held a consultation with my wife and children and finally got rid of the heavy burden.

I knew that I should have some difficulty in persuading my wife, and I was sure that I should have none so far as the children were concerned. So I decided to constitute them my pleaders.

The children readily agreed to my proposal. 'We do not need these costly presents, we must return them to the community, and should we ever need them, we could easily purchase them,' they said.

I was delighted. 'Then you will plead with mother, won't you?' I asked them.

'Certainly,' said they. 'That is our business. She does not need to wear the ornaments. She would want to keep them for us, and if we don't want them, why should she not agree to part with them?'

But it was easier said than done.

"You may not need them,' said my wife. 'Your children may not need them. Cajoled they will dance to your tune. I can understand your not permitting me to wear them. But what about my daughters-in-law? They will be sure to need them. And who knows what will happen tomorrow? I would be the last person to part with gifts so lovingly given.'

And thus the torrent of argument went on, strengthened in the end by tears. But I was determined to return the ornaments. I somehow succeeded in the end in extorting a consent from her. The gifts received in 1896 and 1901 were all returned. A trust-deed was prepared, and they were deposited with a bank, to be used for the service of the community, according to my wishes or to those of the trustees.

I have never since regretted the step, and as the years have gone by, my wife has also seen its wisdom. It has saved us from many temptations.

I am definitely of the opinion that a public worker should accept no costly gifts.

Back in India

My First Congress

After reaching India I spent some time in going about the country. It was the year 1901 when the Congress met at Calcutta under the presidentship of Mr (later Sir) Dinshaw Wacha. And I of course attended it. It was my first experience of the Congress.

I asked a volunteer where I was to go. He took me to the Ripon College, where a number of delegates were being put up. The volunteers were clashing against one another. You asked one of them to do something. He sent you to another, and he in his turn to a third and so on; and as for the delegates, they were neither here nor there.

There was no limit to insanitation. Pools of water were everywhere. There were only a few latrines, and the recollection of their stink still oppresses me. I pointed it out to the volunteers. They said point blank: 'That is not our work, it is the scavenger's work.' I asked for a broom. The man stared at me in wonder. I got one and cleaned the latrine. But that was for myself. The rush was so great, and the latrines were so few, that they needed frequent cleaning; but that was more than I could do.

There were yet two days for the Congress session to begin. I had made up my mind to offer my services to the Congress office in order to gain some experience. Babu Bhupendranath Basu and Sjt. Ghosal were the secretaries. I went to Bhupenbabu and offered my services. He looked at me, and said: 'I have no work, but possibly Ghosalbabu might have something to give you. Please go to him.'

So I went to him. He looked at me and said with a smile: 'I can give you only clerical work. Will you do it?'

'Certainly,' said I. 'I am here to do anything that is not beyond my capacity.'

Shri Ghosal used to get his shirt buttoned by his bearer. I volunteered to do the bearer's duty, and I loved to do it, as my regard for elders was always great. When he came to know this, he did not mind my doing little acts of personal service for him. In fact he was delighted. The benefit I received from this service is incalculable.

In a few days, I came to know the working of the Congress. I met most of the leaders.

Sir Pherozeshah had agreed to admit my resolution on South Africa, but I was wondering who would put it before the Subjects Committee, and when. For there were lengthy speeches to every resolution all in English and every resolution had some well-known leader to back it. As the night was closing in, my heart beat fast. Everyone was hurrying to go. It was 11 o'clock. I had not the courage to speak. I had already met Gokhale, who had looked at my resolution. So I drew near his chair and whispered to him: 'Please do something for me.'

'So we have done?' said Sir Pherozeshah Mehta.

'No, no, there is still the resolution on South Africa. Mr Gandhi has been waiting long,' cried out Gokhale.

'Have you seen the resolution?' asked Sir Pherozeshah.

'Of course.'

'Do you like it?'

'It is quite good.'

'Well then, let us have it, Gandhi.'

I read it trembling.

Gokhale supported it.

'Unanimously passed,' cried out everyone.

'You will have five minutes to speak to it Gandhi,' said Mr Wacha.

The procedure was far from pleasing to me. No one had troubled to understand the resolution, everyone was in a hurry to go and because Gokhale had seen the resolution, it was not thought necessary for the rest to see it or understand it!

And yet the very fact that it was passed by the Congress was enough to delight my heart. The knowledge that the approval of the Congress meant that of the whole country was enough to delight anyone.

In Bombay

Gokhale was very anxious that I should settle down in Bombay, practise at the bar and help in public work.

I prospered in my profession better than I had expected. My South African clients often entrusted me with some work, and it was enough to enable me to pay my way.

Just when I seemed to be settling down as I had intended, I received an unexpected cable from South Africa: 'Chamberlain expected here. Please return immediately.' I remembered my promise and cabled to say that I should be ready to start the moment they sent me money. They promptly responded. I gave up the chambers and started for South Africa.

In South Africa Again

In South Africa Again

I reached Durban not a day too soon. There was work waiting for me. The date for the deputation to wait on Mr Chamberlain had been fixed. I had to draft the memorial to be submitted to him and accompany the deputation.

Mr Chamberlain, however, gave a cold shoulder to the Indian deputation.

'You know,' he said, 'that the Imperial Government has little control over self-governing Colonies. Your grievances seem to be genuine. I shall do what I can, but you must try your best to placate the Europeans, if you wish to live in their midst.'

The reply cast a chill over the members of the deputation. I was also disappointed. It was an eye-opener for us all, and I saw that we should start with our work afresh. I explained the situation to my colleagues.

I added: 'To tell you the truth, the work for which you had called me is practically finished. But I believe I ought not to leave the Transvaal, so far as it is possible, even if you permit me to return home. Instead of carrying on my work from Natal, as before, I must now do so from here. I must no longer think of returning to India within a year, but must get enrolled in the Transvaal Supreme Court. I have confidence enough to deal with this new department. If we do not do this, the community will be driven out of the country.'

So I set the ball rolling, discussed things with Indians in Pretoria and Johannesburg, and ultimately decided to set up office in Johannesburg.

Study of the *Gita*

I already had faith in the *Gita*, which had a fascination for me. Now I realized the necessity of diving deeper into it. I had one or two translations, by means of which I tried to understand the original Sanskrit. I decided also to learn by heart one or two verses every day. For this purpose I employed the time of my morning ablutions. The operation took me thirty-five minutes, fifteen minutes for the toothbrush and twenty for the bath. So on the wall opposite I stuck slips of paper on which were written the *Gita* verses and referred to them now and then to help my memory. This time was found sufficient for memorizing the daily portion and recalling the verses already learnt. I remember having thus committed to memory thirteen chapters.

To me the *Gita* became the guide of conduct. It became my dictionary of daily reference. Words like *aparigraha* (non-possession) and *samabhava* (equability) gripped me. How to cultivate and preserve that equability was the question. Was I to give up all I had and follow Him? Straight came the answer: I could not follow Him unless I gave up all I had. I then wrote to Ravishankerbhai to allow the insurance policy to lapse and get whatever could be recovered, or else to regard the premiums already paid as lost, for I had become convinced that God, who created my wife and children as well as myself, would take care of them. To my brother, who had been as a father to me, I wrote explaining that I had given him all that I had saved up to that moment, but that henceforth he should expect nothing from me, for future savings, if any, would be utilized for the benefit of the community.

The Magic Spell of a Book

Mr Polak, a friend of mine, came to see me off to Durban, and left with me a book to read during the journey, which he said I was sure to like. It was Ruskin's *Unto This Last*.

The book was impossible to lay aside, once I had begun it. It gripped me. Johannesburg to Durban was a twenty-four hours' journey. The train reached there in the evening. I could not get any sleep that night. I determined to change my life in accordance with the ideals of the book.

I believe that I discovered some of my deepest convictions reflected in this great book of Ruskin, and that is why it so captured me and made me transform my life.

The teaching of *Unto This Last* I understood to be:

That the good of the individual is contained in the good of all.

That a lawyer's work has the same value as the barber's inasmuch as all have the same right of earning their livelihood from their work.

That a life of labour, i.e. the life of the tiller of the soil and the handicraftsman is the life worth living.

The first of these I knew. The second I had dimly realized. The third had never occurred to me. *Unto This Last* made it as clear as daylight for me that the second and the third were contained in the first. I arose with the dawn, ready to reduce these principles to practice.

The Phoenix Settlement

I talked over the whole thing with Mr West, who was in charge of the printing of *Indian Opinion*, which was a weekly paper that I was running, described to him the effect *Unto This Last* had produced on my mind, and proposed that *Indian Opinion* should be removed to a farm, on which everyone should labour, drawing the same living wage, and attending to the press work in spare time. Mr West approved of the proposal, and £3 was laid down as the monthly allowance per head, irrespective of colour or nationality.

Thus the Phoenix Settlement was started in 1904 and there in spite of numerous odds *Indian Opinion* continued to be published.

I had now given up all hope of returning to India in the near future. I had promised my wife that I would return home within a year. The year was gone without any prospect of my return, so I decided to send for her and the children.

The Zulu Rebellion

Just when I felt that I should be breathing in peace, an unexpected event happened. The papers brought the news of the outbreak of the Zulu 'rebellion' in Natal. I bore no grudge against the Zulus, they had harmed no Indian. I had doubts about the 'rebellion' itself. But I then believed that the British Empire existed for the welfare of the world. Natal had a Volunteer Defence Force.

I considered myself a citizen of Natal, being intimately connected with it. So I wrote to the Governor, expressing my readiness, if necessary, to form an Indian Ambulance Corps. He replied immediately accepting the offer.

I went to Durban and appealed for men. In order to give me a status and to facilitate work, as also in accordance with the existing convention, the Chief Medical Officer appointed me to the temporary rank of Sergeant Major and three men selected by me to the ranks of sergeants and one to that of corporal. We also received our uniforms from the Government. Our Corps was on active service for nearly six weeks. Our main work was to be the nursing of the wounded Zulus. The Medical Officer in charge welcomed us. He said the white people were not willing nurses for the wounded Zulus, that their wounds were festering, and that he was at his wits' end. He hailed our arrival as a godsend for those innocent people.

Kasturba's Courage

A medical friend once advised a surgical operation for my wife, to which she agreed after some hesitation. She was getting very thin, and the doctor had to perform the operation without chloroform. It was successful, but she had to suffer much pain. She, however, went through it with wonderful bravery. The doctor and his wife who nursed her were all attention. This was in Durban. The doctor gave me leave to go to Johannesburg, and told me not to have any anxiety about the patient.

In a few days, however, I received a letter to the effect that Kasturba was worse, too weak to sit up in bed, and had once become unconscious. The doctor knew that he might not, without my consent, give her wines or meat. So he telephoned me at Johannesburg for permission to give her beef tea. I replied saying that I could not grant the permission, but that, if she was in a condition to express her wish in the matter she might be consulted and she was free to do as she liked. 'But,' said the doctor, 'I refuse to consult the patient's wishes in the matter. You must come yourself. If you do not leave me free to prescribe whatever diet I like, I will not hold myself responsible for your wife's life.'

I took the train for Durban the same day, and met the doctor who quietly broke this news to me: 'I had already given Mrs Gandhi beef tea when I telephoned you.'

'Now, doctor, I call this a fraud,' said I.

'No question of fraud in prescribing medicine or diet for a patient. In fact, we doctors consider it a virtue to deceive patients or their relatives, if thereby we can save our patients,' said the doctor with determination.

I was deeply pained, but kept cool. The doctor was a good man and a personal friend. He and his wife had laid me under a debt of gratitude, but I was not prepared to put up with his medical morals.

'Doctor, tell me what you propose to do now. I would never allow my wife to be given meat or beef, even if the denial meant her death, unless of course she desired to take it.'

'You are welcome to your philosophy. I tell you that, so long as you keep your wife under my treatment, I must have the option to give her anything I wish. If you don't like this, I must regretfully ask you to remove her. I can't see her die under my roof.'

I think one of my sons was with me. He entirely agreed with me, and said his mother should not be given beef tea. I next spoke to Kasturba herself. She was really too weak to be consulted in this matter. But I thought it my painful duty to do so. I told her what had passed between the doctor and myself. She gave a firm reply: 'I will not take beef tea. It is a rare thing in this world to be born as a human being, and I would far rather die in your arms than pollute my body with such abominations.'

I pleaded with her. I told her that she was not bound to follow me. I cited to her the instances of Hindu friends and acquaintances who had no scruples about taking meat or wine as medicine. But she was adamant. 'No,' said she, 'pray remove me at once.'

So we decided to leave the place at once. It was drizzling and the station was some distance. We had to take the train from Durban for Phoenix, whence our Settlement was reached by a road of two miles and a half. I was undoubtedly taking a very great risk, but I trusted in God, and proceeded with my task.

IN SOUTH AFRICA AGAIN

I sent a messenger to Phoenix in advance, with a message to West to receive us at the station with a hammock, a bottle of hot milk and one of hot water, and six men to carry Kasturba in the hammock. I got a rickshaw to enable me to take her by the next available train, put her into it in that dangerous condition, and marched away.

Kasturba needed no cheering up. On the contrary, she comforted me, saying: 'Nothing will happen to me. Don't worry.'

She was mere skin and bone, having had no nourishment for days. The station platform was very large and as the rickshaw could not be taken inside, one had to walk some distance before one could reach the train. So I carried her in my arms and put her into the compartment. From Phoenix we carried her in the hammock, and there she slowly picked up strength under water-cure treatment.

Domestic Satyagraha

Now it happened that Kasturba, who was well for a brief period after her operation, fell ill again. She had not much faith in my remedies, though she did not resist them. She certainly did not ask for outside help. So when all my remedies had failed, I entreated her to give up salt and pulses. She would not agree, however much I pleaded with her, supporting myself with authorities. At last, she challenged me, saying that even I could not give up these articles if I was advised to do so. I was pained and equally delighted – delighted in that I got an opportunity to shower my love on her. I said to her: 'You are mistaken. If I was ailing and the doctor advised me to give up these or any other articles, I should unhesitatingly do so. But there! Without any medical advice, I give up salt and pulses for one year, whether you do so or not.'

She was rudely shocked and exclaimed in deep sorrow: 'Pray forgive me. Knowing you, I should not have provoked you. I promise to go without these things, but for heaven's sake take back your vow. This is too hard on me.'

'It is very good for you to forego these articles. I have not the slightest doubt that you will be all the better without them. As for me, I cannot go back on a vow seriously taken. And it is sure to benefit me, for all restraint, whatever prompts it, is wholesome for men. You will therefore leave me alone. It will be a test for me, and a moral support to you in carrying out your resolve.'

So she gave up. 'You are too obstinate. You will listen to none,' she said, and sought relief in tears. I would like to count this incident as an instance of Satyagraha, and it is one of the sweetest recollections of my life. After this, Kasturba began to pick up quickly.

The Advent of Satyagraha

On return from duty in connection with the Zulu 'Rebellion' I met the friends at Phoenix and reached Johannesburg. Here I read with deep horror the draft Ordinance published in the Transvaal Government Gazette Extraordinary of August 22, 1906. It meant absolute ruin for Indians in South Africa. Under it every Indian, man, woman or child, of eight years or upwards, entitled to reside in the Transvaal, must register his or her name with the Registrar of Asiatics and take out a

IN SOUTH AFRICA AGAIN

certificate of registration. The applicants for registration must surrender their old permits to the Registrar and state in their applications their name, residence, caste, age etc. The Registrar was to note down important marks of identification upon the applicant's person, and take his finger and thumb impressions. Every Indian who failed thus to apply for registration before a certain date was to give up his right of residence in the Transvaal. Failure to apply would be held to be an offence in law for which a person could be fined, sent to prison or even sent away from the country. Even a person walking on public thoroughfares could be required to produce his certificate. Police officers could enter private houses in order to inspect certificates. I have never known legislation of this nature being directed against free men in any part of the world.

The next day, a small meeting of leading Indians was held to whom I explained the Ordinance word by word. It shocked them as it had shocked me. All present realized the seriousness of the situation and resolved to hold a public meeting.

The meeting was duly held on September 11, 1906. The most important among the resolutions passed by the meeting was the famous Fourth Resolution, by which the Indians solemnly determined not to submit to the Ordinance in the event of its becoming law in the teeth of their opposition, and to suffer all the penalties attaching to such non-submission.

None of us knew what name to give to our movement. Shri Maganlal Gandhi suggested the word 'Sadagraha', meaning 'firmness in a good cause'. I liked the word, but it did not fully represent the whole idea I wished it to convey. I therefore corrected it to 'Satyagraha'. Truth *(satya)* implies love, and firmness *(agraha)* brings about and therefore serves as a synonym for force. I thus began to call the Indian movement 'Satyagraha', that is to say, the force which is born of Truth and Love or non-violence, and gave up the use of the phrase 'passive resistance', in connection with it.

Imprisonment

The officers of the Asiatic Department came to think the strength of the movement could not by any means be broken so long as certain leaders were at large. So they arrested some of us.

The community had resolved to fill up the jail after our arrests.

We had been in jail for a fortnight, when fresh arrivals brought the news that there were going on some negotiations about a compromise with the Government. The substance of the proposed settlement was that the Indians should register voluntarily and that if the majority of the Indians underwent voluntary registration, Government should repeal the Black Act, as the Asiatic Registration Act came to be called.

I was taken to Pretoria to meet General Smuts and after discussion with him of an amendment I had suggested, the draft settlement was accepted. The prisoners were released and I went about explaining the terms of the settlement to my countrymen.

Assault

A couple of Pathans were angry with me for consenting to the giving of fingerprints. It had been agreed that the leaders should be the first to take out certificates on the first day. When I reached my office, which was also the office of the Satyagraha Association, I found Mir Alam, a Pathan, and his companions standing outside the premises. Mir Alam was an old client of mine, and used to seek my advice in all his affairs. He was fully six feet in height and of a large and powerful build. Today, for the first time, I saw Mir Alam outside my office instead of inside it, and although his eyes met mine, he for the first time did not salute me. I saluted him and he saluted me in return. But he did not today wear his usual smile. I noticed his angry eyes and took a mental note of the fact. I thought that something was going to happen. The chairman, Mr Yusuf Mian and other friends arrived, and we set out for the Asiatic Office. Mir Alam and his companions followed us.

As we were not more than three minutes' walk from the Registration Office, Mir Alam came up to me and asked me, 'Where are you going?'

'I propose to take out a certificate of registration, giving the ten finger-prints,' I replied. 'If you will go with me, I will first get you a certificate with an impression only of the two thumbs, and then I will take one for myself, giving the finger-prints.'

I had scarcely finished the last sentence when a heavy cudgel blow descended on my head from behind. I at once fainted with the words *He Rama* (O God!) on my lips, lay flat on the ground and had no notion of what followed. But Mir Alam and his companions gave me more blows and kicks, some of which were warded off by Yusuf Mian and Thambi Naidoo with the result that they too were beaten in their turn.

The noise attracted some European passers-by to the scene. Mir Alam and his companions fled but were caught by the Europeans. The police arrived in the meanwhile and took them away. I was picked up and carried into Mr J.C. Gibson's private office. When I regained consciousness, I saw Mr Doke bending over me. 'How do you feel?' he asked me.

'I am all right,' I replied, 'but there is pain in the teeth and the ribs. Where is Mir Alam?'

'He has been arrested along with the rest.'

'They should be released.'

'That is all very well. But here you are in a stranger's office with your lip and cheek badly torn. The police are ready to take you to the hospital, but if you will go to my place, Mrs Doke and I will look after you as best as we can.'

'Yes, please take me to your place. Thank the police for their offer but tell them that I prefer to go with you.'

Mr Chamney, the Registrar of the Asiatic Office, too now arrived on the scene. I was taken in a carriage to this good clergy-man's residence in Smit Street and a doctor was called in. Meanwhile I said to Mr Chamney: 'I wished to come to your office, give ten finger-prints and take out the first certificate of registration, but God willed it otherwise. However, I have now to request you to bring the papers and allow me to register at once. I hope that you will not let anyone else register before me.'

'Where is the hurry about it?' asked Mr Chamney. 'The doctor will be here soon. You please rest yourself and all will be well. I will issue certificate to others but keep your name at the head of the list.'

IN SOUTH AFRICA AGAIN

'Not so,' I replied. 'I am pledged to take out the first certificate if I am alive and if it is acceptable to God. It is therefore that I insist upon the papers being brought here and now.'

Upon this Mr Chamney went away to bring the papers.

The second thing for me to do was to write to the Attorney-General that I did not hold Mir Alam and others guilty for the assault committed upon me, that in any case I did not wish them to be prosecuted and that I hoped they would be let off for my sake. But the Europeans of Johannesburg addressed a strong letter to the Attorney-General saying that whatever views Gandhi might hold as regards the punishment of criminals, they could not be given effect to in South Africa. Gandhi himself might not take any steps, but the assault was committed not in a private place but on the high roads and was therefore public offence. Several Englishmen too were in a position to tender evidence and the offenders must be prosecuted. Upon this, the Attorney-General re-arrested Mir Alam and one of his companions who were sentenced to three months' hard labour. Only I was not summoned as a witness.

I addressed a short note as follows to the community through the Chairman and sent it for publication:

'I am well in the brotherly and sisterly hands of Mr and Mrs Doke. I hope to take up my duty shortly.

'Those who have committed the act did not know what they were doing. They thought that I was doing what was wrong. They have had their revenge in the only manner they know. I therefore request that no steps be taken against them.'

Mr Chamney returned with the papers and I gave my finger-prints but not without pain. I then saw that tears stood in Mr Chamney's eyes. I had often to write bitterly against him, but this showed me how man's heart may be softened by events.

Resumption of Satyagraha

The Indians had registered voluntarily. The Government were, therefore, on their part to repeal the Black Act. But instead of repealing the Black Act, General Smuts maintained the Black Act on the statute book and introduced into the legislature a measure, 'making further provision for the registration of Asiatics': I was shocked when I read the Bill.

An 'Ultimatum' was sent to the Government by the Satyagrahis. It said in effect, 'If the Asiatic Act is not repealed, the certificates collected by the Indians would be burnt, and they would humbly but firmly take the consequences.'

A meeting had been called to perform the public ceremony of burning the certificates.

As the business of the meeting was about to commence, a volunteer arrived on a cycle with a telegram from the Government in which they regretted the determination of the Indian community and announced their inability to change their line of action. The telegram was read to the audience which received it with cheers, as if they were glad that the auspicious opportunity of burning the certificates did not after all slip out of their hands.

Mir Alam too was present at this meeting. He announced that he had done wrong to assault me as he did, and to the great joy of the audience, handed his original certificate to be burnt, as he had not taken a voluntary certificate. I took hold of his hand, pressed it with joy, and assured him once more that I had never had in my mind any resentment against him.

The Committee had already received upwards of 2,000 certificates to be burnt. These were all thrown into the fire, soaked with kerosene oil and set ablaze by Mr Yusuf Mian. The whole assembly rose to their feet and made the place resound with the echoes of their continuous cheers during the burning process. Some of those who had still withheld their certificates brought them in numbers to the platform, and these too were thrown to the flames.

The reporters of English newspapers present at the meeting were profoundly impressed with the whole scene and gave vivid descriptions of the meeting in their papers.

During the same year in which the Black Act was passed General Smuts carried through the Legislature another Bill called the Transvaal Immigrants Restriction Bill. This Act indirectly prevented the entry of a single Indian newcomer into the Transvaal.

It was absolutely essential for the Indians to resist this fresh inroad on their rights. Several Satyagrahis therefore deliberately entered the Transvaal and were imprisoned. I too was arrested again.

Gokhale came to South Africa in October 1912 to mediate between the Satyagrahis and the Government. General Botha, according to Gokhale, promised him that the Black Act would be repealed in a year and the £3 tax abolished. But this was not done.

I wrote to Gokhale about the breach of the pledge and set about making preparations for the ensuing campaign.

Till now we had dissuaded women from courting imprisonment. But at this time judgement was passed by the South African Government which made invalid all marriages that had not been celebrated according to Christian rites and registered by the Registrar of Marriages. Thus at a stroke of the pen all marriages celebrated according to Hindu, Mussalman and Zoroastrian rites became illegal, and the wives concerned were degraded to the rank of concubines and their children deprived of the right to inherit property. This was an unbearable situation for women no less than men.

Patience was impossible in the place of this insult offered to our womanhood. We decided to offer stubborn Satyagraha irrespective of the number of fighters. Not only could the women now not be prevented from joining the struggle, but we decided even to invite them to come into line along with the men.

The women's imprisonment worked like a charm upon the labourers on the mines near Newcastle who downed their tools and entered the city in succeeding batches. As soon as I received the news, I left Phoenix for Newcastle.

The labourers were not to be counted by tens but by hundreds. And their number might easily swell into thousands. How was I to house and feed this ever-growing multitude? There was a huge gathering of men, which was continuously increasing. It was a dangerous if not an impossible task to keep them in one place and look after them while they had no employment. I thought out a solution of my problem. I must take this 'army' to the Transvaal and see them safely deposited in jail. The strength of the 'army' was about five thousand.

The Triumph of Satyagraha

The Union Government had not the power to keep thousands of innocent men in jail. The Viceroy would not tolerate it, and all the world was waiting to see what General Smuts would do. The Union Government now did what all governments similarly situated generally do. They get out of such awkward situation by appointing a commission. It is a general practice that the recommendations of such a commission should be accepted by the State, and therefore under the guise of carrying out the recommendations, governments give the justice which they have first refused. General Smuts appointed a commission of three members.

I entered into correspondence with General Smuts over the work of the commission and came to an agreement. The commission in its report recommended acceptance of the demands of the Indian community; and within a short time after the issue of the report, the Government published in the official Gazette of the Union the Indians' Relief Bill which abolished the £3 tax, made legal all marriages deemed legal in India, and made a domicile certificate bearing the holder's thumb-print sufficient evidence of the right to enter the Union.

Thus the great Satyagraha struggle closed after eight years, and it appeared that the Indians in South Africa were now at peace. On July 18, 1914, I sailed for England on my way back to India. It was difficult for me to leave South Africa, where I had passed twenty-one years of my life sharing to the full in the sweets and bitters of human experience and where I had realized my calling in life.

In India and Founding of the Ashram

In Poona

It was a joy to get back to the homeland after so many years of exile.

Gokhale and the members of the Servants of India Society[7] overwhelmed me with affection. So far as I recollect, Gokhale got all of them together to meet me. I had a frank talk with them all on every sort of subject.

---

7 Founded by Gokhale and consisting of men pledged to devote all their lives to the service of the country on such allowances as the society may be able to give. Its work covered many fields—political, social, economic and educational; moderate in politics, it was a non-communal organisation which did not recognize caste distinctions. It conducted several institutions throughout the country.

I wanted to have an Ashram where I could settle down with my Phoenix family, preferably somewhere in Gujarat, as being a Gujarati, I thought I was best fitted to serve the country through serving Gujarat. Gokhale liked the idea. He said: 'You should certainly do so. You must look to me for the expenses of the Ashram, which I will regard as my own.'

My heart overflowed with joy. It was a pleasure to feel free from the responsibility of raising funds.

Founding of the Ashram

The Satyagraha Ashram was founded on the 25th of May, 1915 at Kochrab in Ahmedabad.

We were in all about twenty-five men and women. All had their meals in a common kitchen and strove to live as one family.

The Ashram had been in existence only a few months when we were put to a test such as I had scarcely expected. I received a letter from Amritlal Thakkar to this effect: 'A humble and honest untouchable family is desirous of joining your Ashram. Will you accept them?'

I wrote to Amritlal Thakkar expressing our willingness to accept the family, provided all the members were ready to abide by the rules of the Ashram.

They all agreed to abide by the rules and were accepted.

But their admission created a stir amongst the friends who had been helping the Ashram. The very first difficulty was found with regard to the use of the well, which was partly controlled by the owner of the bungalow. The man in charge of the water-lift objected that drops of water from our bucket would pollute him. So he took to swearing at us. I told everyone to put up with the abuse and continue drawing water at any cost. When he saw that we did not return his abuse, the man became ashamed and ceased to bother us.

All monetary help, however, was stopped. With the stopping of monetary help came rumours of proposed social boycott. We were prepared for all this. I had told my companions that, if we were boycotted and denied the usual facilities, we would not leave Ahmedabad. We would rather go and stay in the 'untouchables' quarter and live on whatever we could get by manual labour.

Matters came to such a pass that Maganlal Gandhi one day gave me this notice: 'We are out of funds and there is nothing for the next month.'

I quietly replied: 'Then we shall go to the "untouchables" quarter.'

This was not the first time I had been faced with such a trial. On all such occasions God had sent help at the last moment. One morning shortly after Maganlal had given me warning of our monetary plight, one of the children came and said that a Sheth who was waiting in a car outside wanted to see me. I went out to him. 'I want to give the Ashram some help. Will you accept it?' he asked.

'Most certainly,' said I. 'And I confess I am at the present moment at the end of my resources.'

'I shall come tomorrow at this time,' he said. 'Will you be here?'

'Yes,' said I, and he left.

Next day, exactly at the appointed hour, the car drew up near our quarters, and the horn was blown. The children came with the news. The Sheth did not come in. I went out to see him. He placed in my hands currency notes of the value of Rs 13,000 and drove away.

I had never expected this help, and what a novel way of rendering it! The gentleman had never before visited the Ashram. So far as I can remember, I had met him only once. No visit, no inquiries, simply rendering help and going away! This was a unique experience for me. We now felt quite safe for a year.

Champaran

The Stain of Indigo

The Champaran tenant was bound by law to plant three out of every twenty parts of his land with indigo for his landlord. This system was known as *tinkathia* system, as three *kathas* out of twenty (which make one acre) had to be planted with indigo.

Rajkumar Shukla was one of the agriculturists who had suffered under this system. He wanted me personally to visit Champaran and see the miseries of the ryots there.

So early in 1917 we left Calcutta for Champaran. My object was to inquire into the condition of the Champaran agriculturists and understand their grievances against the indigo planters. For this purpose it was necessary that I should meet thousands of the ryots. But I thought it essential, before starting on my inquiry, to know the planters' side of the case and see the Commissioner of the Division. I sought and was granted appointments with both.

The Secretary of the Planters' Association told me plainly that I was an outsider and that I had no business to come between the planters and their tenants, but if I had any representation to make, I might submit it in writing. I politely told him that I did not regard myself as an outsider, and that I had every right to inquire into the condition of the tenants if they desired me to do so.

The Commissioner, on whom I called, advised me forthwith to leave Tirhut.

I acquainted my co-workers with all this, and told them that there was a likelihood of Government stopping me from proceeding further, and that I might have to go to jail earlier than I had expected, and if I was to be arrested, it would be best that the arrest should take place in Motihari or if possible in Bettiah. It was advisable, therefore, that I should go to those places as early as possible.

Champaran is a district of the Tirhut division in Bihar, and Motihari is its headquarters. Rajkumar Shukla's place was in the vicinity of Bettiah, and the tenants in its neighbourhood were the poorest in the district. Rajkumar Shukla wanted me to see them and I was equally anxious to do so.

So I started with my co-workers for Motihari the same day. The very same day we heard that about five miles from Motihari a tenant had been ill-treated. It was decided that, in company with Babu Dharanidhar Prasad, I should go and see him the next morning, and we accordingly set off for the place on elephant's back. We had scarcely gone halfway when

CHAMPARAN

a messenger from the Police Superintendent overtook us and said that the latter had sent his compliments. I saw what he meant. Having left Dharanidhar Babu to proceed to the original destination, I got into the hired carriage which the messenger had brought. He then served on me a notice to leave Champaran, and drove me to my place. On his asking me to acknowledge the service of the notice, I wrote to the effect that I did not propose to leave Champaran till my inquiry was finished. Thereupon I received a summons to take my trial the next day for disobeying the order to leave Champaran.

The news of the notice and the summons spread like wildfire, and I was told that Motihari that day witnessed unprecedented scenes. Gorakhbabu's house and the courthouse overflowed with men. Fortunately I had finished all my work during the night and so was able to manage the crowds. My companions proved the greatest help. They occupied themselves with regulating the crowds, for the latter followed me wherever I went.

A sort of friendliness sprang up between the officials—Collector, Magistrate, Police Superintendent—and myself. I might have legally resisted the notices served on me. Instead, I accepted them all, and my conduct towards the officials was correct. They thus saw that I did not want to offend them personally, but that I wanted to offer civil resistance to their orders. In this way they were put at ease, and instead of harassing me they gladly availed themselves of my and my co-workers' cooperation in regulating the crowds. But it was a visible demonstration to them of the fact that their authority was shaken. The people had for the moment lost all fear of punishment and yielded obedience to the power of love which their new friends exercised.

It should be remembered that no one knew me in Champaran. And yet they received me as though we had been age-old friends. It is no exaggeration, but the literal truth, to say that in this meeting with the peasants I was face to face with God, Ahimsa, and Truth.

That day in Champaran was an unforgettable event in my life and a red-letter day for the peasants and for me.

The trial began. The Government pleader, the Magistrate and other officials were at a loss to know what to do.

Before I could appear before the Court to receive the sentence, the Magistrate sent a written message that the Lieutenant Governor had ordered the case against me to be withdrawn, and the Collector wrote to me saying that I was at liberty to conduct the proposed inquiry, and that I might count on whatever help I needed from the officials. None of us was prepared for this prompt and happy issue.

Crowds of peasants came to make their statements, and they were followed by an army of companions who filled the compound and garden to overflowing.

The Stain Removed

The ever growing number of ryots coming to make their statements increased the planters' wrath, and they moved heaven and earth to put an end to my inquiry.

But Sir Edward Gait, the Lieutenant Governor, asked me to see him, expressed his willingness to appoint an inquiry and invited me to be a member of the Committee.

The Committee voted in favour of the ryots, and recommended that the planters should refund a portion of the exactions made by them which the Committee had found to be unlawful, and that the *tinkathia* system should be abolished by law.

The *tinkathia* system which had been in existence for about a century was thus abolished, and with it the planters' raj came to an end.

Ahmedabad Labour

In Touch with Labour

At this time there came a letter from Shrimati Anasuyabehn about the condition of labour in Ahmedabad. Wages were low, the labourers had long been agitating for an increment, and I had a desire to guide them if I could. So I went to Ahmedabad.

I was in a most delicate situation. The mill-hands' case was strong. Shrimad Anasuyabehn had to battle against her own brother, Shri Ambalal Sarabhai, who led the fight on behalf of the mill-owners. My relations with them were friendly, and that made fighting with them more difficult. I held consultations with them, and requested them to refer the dispute to arbitration, but they refused to recognize the principle of arbitration.

I had therefore to advise the labourers to go on strike. Before I did so, I came in very close contact with them and their leaders, and explained to them the conditions of a successful strike:

1 never to resort to violence,
2 never to molest blacklegs,
3 never to depend upon alms, and
4 to remain firm, no matter how long the strike continued, and to earn bread, during the strike, by any other honest labour.

The leaders of the strike understood and accepted the conditions, and the labourers pledged themselves at a general meeting not to resume work until either their terms were accepted or the mill-owners agreed to refer the dispute to arbitration.

For the first two weeks the mill-hands exhibited great courage and self-restraint and daily held large meetings. On these occasions I used to remind them of their pledge, and they would shout back to me the assurance that they would rather die than break their word.

But later they began to show signs of weakening. I felt deeply troubled and began thinking hard as to what my duty was in the circumstances.

One morning—it was at a mill-hands' meeting—while I was still groping and unable to see my way clearly, the light came to me. Unbidden and all by themselves the words came to my lips: 'Unless the strikers rally,' I declared to the meeting, 'and continue the strike till a settlement is reached, or till they leave the mills altogether, I will not touch any food.'

The labourers were thunderstruck. Tears began to course down Anasuyabehn's cheeks. The labourers broke out, 'Not you but we shall fast. It would be monstrous if you were to fast. Please forgive us for our lapse, we will now remain faithful to our pledge to the end.'

'There is no need for you to fast,' I replied. 'It would be enough if you could remain true to your pledge. As you know we are without funds, and we do not want to continue our strike by living on public charity. You should therefore try to earn your bare living by some kind of labour, so that you may be able to remain unconcerned, no matter how long the strike may continue. As for my fast, it will be broken only after the strike is settled.'

Anasuyabehn and a number of other friends and labourers shared the fast with me on the first day. But after some difficulty I was able to dissuade them from continuing it further.

The net result of it was that an atmosphere of goodwill was created all round. The hearts of the mill-owners were touched, and they set about discovering some means for a settlement. Anasuyabehn's house became the meeting place for their discussions. Shri Anandshankar Dhruva intervened and was in the end appointed arbitrator, and the strike was called off after I had fasted only for three days. The mill-owners commemorated the event by distributing sweets among the labourers, and thus a settlement was reached after twenty-one days' strike.

The Kheda Satyagraha

The Kheda Satyagraha

No breathing time was, however, in store for me. Hardly was the Ahmedabad mill-hands' strike over, when I had to plunge into the Kheda Satyagraha struggle.

A condition approaching famine had arisen in the Kheda district owing to a widespread failure of crops, and the Patidars of Kheda were considering the question of getting the Government not to collect its land revenue for the year.

Under the Land Revenue Rules, if the crop was four annas[8] or under, the cultivators could claim full suspension of payment of revenue for the year. According to the official figures the crop was said to be over four annas. The contention of the cultivators, on the other hand, was that it was less than four annas. But the Government was in no mood to listen.

---

8 i.e. four annas in the rupee (16 annas), or one-fourth the normal

At last, all petitioning and prayer having failed, after taking counsel with co-workers, I advised the Patidars to resort to Satyagraha.

In the initial stages, though the people exhibited much courage, the Government did not seem inclined to take strong action. But as the people's firmness showed no signs of wavering, the Government began coercion. The attachment officers sold people's cattle and seized whatever movables they could lay hands on. Penalty notices were served, and in some cases standing crops were attached.

With a view to steeling the hearts of those who were frightened, I advised the people, under the leadership of Shri Mohanlal Pandya, to remove the crop of onion from a field which had been, in my opinion, wrongly attached. This was a good opportunity for the people to learn a lesson in courting fines or imprisonment, which was the necessary consequence of such disobedience. For Shri Mohanlal Pandya it was a thing after his heart. So he volunteered to remove the onion crop from the field, and in this seven or eight friends joined him.

It was impossible for the Government to leave them free. The arrest of Shri Mohanlal and his companions added to the people's, enthusiasm. When the fear of jail disappears, repression puts heart into the people.

A procession escorted the 'convicts' to jail, and on that day Shri Mohanlal Pandya earned from the people the honoured title of *dungli chor* (onion thief) which he enjoys to this day.

I was looking for some graceful way of ending the struggle which would be acceptable to a Satyagrahi. Such a one appeared quite unexpectedly. The Mamlatdar of the Nadiad

THE KHEDA SATYAGRAHA

Taluka sent me word that if well-to-do Patidars paid up, the poorer ones would be permitted not to pay. I asked for a written undertaking to that effect, which was given. I inquired of the Collector, who alone could give an undertaking in respect of the whole district, whether the Mamlatdar's undertaking was true for the whole district. He replied that orders in terms of the Mamlatdar's letter had been already issued. I was not aware of it, but if it was a fact, the people's pledge had been fulfilled. The pledge, it will be remembered, had the same thing for its object, and so we expressed ourselves satisfied with the orders.

The Kheda Satyagraha marks the beginning of an awakening among the peasants of Gujarat, the beginning of their true political education. The lesson became firmly impressed on the public mind that the salvation of the people depends upon themselves, upon the capacity for suffering and sacrifice. Through the Kheda campaign Satyagraha took firm root in the soil of Gujarat.

Near Death's Door

In those days my food principally consisted of groundnut butter and lemons. I knew that it was possible to eat too much butter and injure one's health, and yet I allowed myself to do so. This gave me a slight attack of dysentery.

There was some festival that day, and although I had told Kasturba that I should have nothing for my midday meal, she tempted me and I yielded. As I was under a vow of taking no milk or milk products, she had specially prepared for me a sweet wheat porridge with oil added to it instead of ghee. She had reserved too a bowlful of mung for me. I was fond of these things, and I readily took them, hoping that without coming to grief I should eat just enough to please Kasturba and to satisfy my palate. But the devil had been only waiting for an opportunity. Instead of eating very little, I had my fill of the meal. This was sufficient invitation to the angel of death. Within an hour, the dysentery appeared in acute form.

I would take no medicine, but preferred to suffer the penalty for my folly. I must have had thirty to forty motions in twenty-four hours. I fasted, not taking even fruit juices in the beginning. The appetite had all gone, I felt that I was at death's door.

Whilst I lay thus ever expectant of death, Shankerlal Bankar constituted himself the guardian of my health, and pressed me to consult Dr Dalal. Dr Dalal was called accordingly. His capacity for taking instantaneous decisions captured me.

He said: 'I cannot rebuild your body unless you take milk. If in addition you would take iron and arsenic injections, I would guarantee fully to make you well.'

'You can give me the injections,' I replied, 'but milk is a different question; I have a vow against it.'

'What exactly is the nature of your vow?' the doctor inquired.

I told him the whole history and the reasons behind my vow, how, since I had come to know that the cow and the buffalo were subjected to the process of *phuka*, I had taken a strong disgust for milk. Moreover, I had always held that milk is not the natural diet of man. I had therefore given up its use altogether. Kasturba was standing near my bed listening all the time to this conversation.

THE KHEDA SATYAGRAHA

'But surely you cannot have any objection to goat's milk then,' she said.

The doctor added: 'If you will take goat's milk, it will be enough for me.'

I gave in. My intense eagerness to take up the Satyagraha fight had created in me a strong desire to live, and so I contented myself with adhering to the letter of my vow only, and sacrificed its spirit. For although I had only the milk of the cow and the she-buffalo in mind when I took the vow, by natural implication it covered the milk of all animals. Nor could it be right for me to consume milk at all, so long as I held that milk is not the natural diet of man. Yet knowing all this I agreed to take goat's milk. The memory of this action even now fills me with remorse, and I am constantly thinking how to give up goat's milk. But I cannot yet free myself from that subtlest of temptations, the desire to serve, which still holds me.

Soon after I began taking goat's milk, Dr Dalal performed on me a successful operation. As I was getting better, my desire to live revived, especially because God had kept work in store for me.

The Rowlatt Act and Entrance into Politics

The Rowlatt Act[9]

I had hardly begun to feel my way towards recovery, when I happened casually to read in the papers the Rowlatt Committee's report which had just been published. Its recommendations startled me. I mentioned my apprehensions to Vallabhbhai, who used to come to see me almost daily. 'Something must be done,' said I to him. 'But what can we do in the circumstances?' he asked in reply. I answered, 'If even a handful of men can be found to sign the pledge of resistance, and the proposed measure is passed into law in defiance of

---

9 This act was passed in 1919 to provide special powers to the Government to suppress movements aimed against the State. It authorized arrest and detention, without trial, of persons suspected of and-government activities.

it, we ought to offer Satyagraha at once. If I was not laid up like this, I should give battle against it all alone, and expect others to follow suit. But in my present helpless condition I feel myself to be altogether unequal to the task.'

The Bill had not yet been gazetted as an Act. I was in a very weak condition, but when I received an invitation from Madras I decided to take the risk of the long journey. Rajagopalachari had then only recently left Salem to settle down for legal practice in Madras. We daily discussed together plans of the fight, but beyond the holding of public meetings I could not then think of any other programme.

While we were engaged thus, news was received that the Rowlatt Bill had been published as an Act. That night I fell asleep while thinking over the question. Towards the small hours of the morning I woke up somewhat earlier than usual. I was still in that twilight condition between sleep and consciousness when suddenly the idea came to me – it was as if in a dream. Early in the morning I related the whole story to Rajagopalachari.

'The idea came to me last night in a dream that we should call upon the country to observe a general *hartal*. Satyagraha is a process of self-purification, and ours is a sacred fight, and it seems to me to be in the fitness of things that it should be begun with an act of self-purification. Let all the people of India, therefore, stop their business on that day and observe the day as one of fasting and prayer.'

Rajagopalachari was at once taken up with my suggestion. Other friends too welcomed it when it was communicated to them later. I drafted a brief appeal. The date of the *hartal* was first fixed on the 30th March 1919, but was later changed to 6th April.

The whole of India from one end to the other, towns as well as villages, observed a complete *hartal* on that day. It was a most wonderful sight.

On the night of the 7th I started for Delhi and Amritsar. Before the train had reached Palwal railway station, I was served with a written order to the effect that I was prohibited from entering the boundary of the Punjab, as my presence there was likely to result in a disturbance of the peace. I was asked by the police to get down from the train. I refused to do so saying, 'I want to go to the Punjab in response to a pressing invitation, not to foment unrest, but to end it. I am therefore sorry that it is not possible for me to comply with this order.'

At Palwal railway station I was taken out of the train and put under police custody. A train from Delhi came in a short time. I was made to enter a third-class carriage, the police party accompanying. On reaching Mathura, I was taken to the police barracks, but no police official could tell me as to what they proposed to do with me or where I was to be taken next. Early at 4 o'clock the next morning, I was woken up and put in a goods train that was going towards Bombay. I was released at Bombay.

There was a great disturbance in the city owing to my arrest. I got into the car. Near Pydhuni[10] I saw that a huge crowd had gathered. On seeing me the people went mad with joy. A procession was immediately formed, and the sky was rent with

---

10 A part of Bombay city

THE ROWLATT ACT AND ENTRANCE INTO POLITICS

the shouts of *Vande Mataram* and *Allaho Akbar*. At Pydhuni we sighted a body of mounted police. Brickbats were raining down from above. I appealed to the crowd to be calm but it seemed as if we should not be able to escape the shower of brickbats. As the procession came out of Abdur Rahman Street and was about to move towards the Crawford Market, it suddenly found itself faced with a body of the mounted police, who had arrived there to prevent it from proceeding further in the direction of the Fort. The crowd was densely packed. It had almost broken through the police cordon. There was hardly any chance of my voice being heard in that vast assembly. Just then the officer in charge of the mounted police gave the order to disperse the crowd, and at once the mounted party charged upon the crowd brandishing their lances as they went. For a moment I felt that I would be hurt. But my fear was groundless, the lances just grazed the car as the lancers swiftly passed by. The ranks of the people were soon broken, and they were thrown into utter confusion, and began to run. Some got trampled under foot, others were badly hurt and crushed. In that seething mass of humanity there was hardly any room for the horses to pass, nor was there any exit by which the people could disperse. So the lancers blindly cut their way through the crowd. I hardly imagine they could see what they were doing. The whole thing presented a most dreadful spectacle. The horsemen and the people were mixed together in mad confusion.

Thus the crowd was dispersed and its progress checked. Our motor was allowed to proceed. I had it stopped before the Commissioner's office, and got down to complain to him about the conduct of the police.

News came of disturbances in Ahmedabad also. I proceeded to Ahmedabad. I learnt that an attempt had been made to pull up the rails near the Nadiad railway station, that a Government officer had been murdered in Viramgam, and that Ahmedabad was under martial law. The people were terror-stricken. They had indulged in acts of violence and were being made to pay for them with interest.

A police officer was waiting at the station to escort me to Mr Pratt, the Commissioner. I found him in a state of rage. I spoke to him gently, and expressed my regret for the disturbances. I suggested that martial law was unnecessary, and declared my readiness to cooperate in all efforts to restore peace. I asked for permission to hold a public meeting on the grounds of the Sabarmati Ashram. The proposal appealed to him, and the meeting was held, I think, on Sunday, the 13th of April, and martial law was withdrawn the same day or the day after. Addressing the meeting, I tried to bring home to the people the sense of their wrong, declared a penitential fast of three days for myself, appealed to the people to go on a similar fast for a day, and suggested to those who had been guilty of acts of violence to confess their guilt.

I saw my duty as clear as daylight. It was unbearable for me to find that the labourers, amongst whom I had spent a good deal of my time, whom I had served and from whom I had expected better things, had taken part in the riots; I felt I was a sharer in their guilt.

I made up my mind to suspend Satyagraha so long as people had not learnt the lesson of peace.

The Birth of Khadi

The Birth of Khadi

When the Satyagraha Ashram was founded at Sabarmati, we introduced a few handlooms there.

The object that we in the Ashram set before ourselves was to be able to clothe ourselves entirely in cloth manufactured by our own hands. We therefore forthwith gave up the use of mill-woven cloth, and all the members of the Ashram resolved to wear hand-woven cloth made from Indian yarn only. By thus adopting cloth woven from mill-yarn as our wear, and propagating it among our friends, we made ourselves voluntary agents of the Indian spinning mills. This in its turn brought us into contact with the mills. We saw that the aim of the mills was more and more to weave the yarn spun by them; their cooperation with the handloom weaver was not willing, but unavoidable and temporary. We became impatient to be able to spin our own yarn. It was clear that, until we could do this ourselves, dependence on the mills would remain. We did not feel that we could render any service to the country by continuing as agents of Indian spinning mills.

We could get neither a spinning wheel nor a spinner to teach us how to spin.

I asked every chance visitor to the Ashram, who was likely to possess some information about hand-spinning, about the art.

In the year 1917 I was taken by my Gujarati friends to preside at the Broach Educational Conference. It was here that I discovered that remarkable lady Gangabehn Majmudar. To her I poured out my grief about the *charkha*, and she lightened my burden by a promise to search for the spinning wheel till she found it.

At last, after no end of wandering in Gujarat, Gangabehn found the spinning wheel in Vijapur in the Baroda State. Quite a number of people there had spinning wheels in their homes, but had long since put them away as useless lumber. They expressed to Gangabehn their readiness to resume spinning, if someone promised to provide them with a regular supply of slivers, and to buy the yarn spun by them. Gangabehn communicated the joyful news to me. The providing of slivers was found to be a difficult task. On my mentioning the thing to the late Umar Sobani, he solved the difficulty by immediately undertaking to send a sufficient supply of slivers from his mill.

I did not like continuously receiving slivers from him. Moreover, it seemed to me to be fundamentally wrong to use mill-slivers. If one could use mill-slivers, why not use mill-

THE BIRTH OF KHADI

yarn as well? Surely no mills supplied slivers to the ancients. How did they make their slivers then? With these thoughts in my mind I suggested to Gangabehn to find carders who could supply slivers. She confidently undertook the task. She engaged a carder who was prepared to card cotton. He demanded thirty-five rupees, if not much more, per month. I considered no price too high at the time. She trained a few youngsters to make slivers out of the carded cotton. Thus the spinning wheel gained a rapid footing in the Ashram.

Farewell

The time has now come to bring these chapters to a close. My life from this point onward has been so public that there is hardly anything about it that people do not know. In fact, my pen instinctively refuses to proceed further. It is not without regret that I have to take leave of the reader. I set a high value on my experiments. I do not know whether I have been able to do justice to them. I can only say that I have spared no pains to give a faithful narrative.

To describe truth as it has appeared to me, has been my ceaseless effort. The exercise has given me great mental peace, because it has been my fond hope that it might bring faith in Truth and Ahimsa to waverers.

Exploring Gandhi in Today's World

Gandhi Around You

Gandhi's influence on India's history and present is undeniable. There are monuments and memorials to the Mahatma across the country that you can visit in order to learn more about his life. Here are just a few museums set up in his honour:

- **Gandhi Smriti and Darshan Samiti, Delhi**

The Gandhi Smriti and Darshan Samiti were founded in 1984. Gandhi Smriti is the house in which Gandhi lived the last days of his life. It is now a museum displaying photographs, artwork and other memorabilia from his life, including his glasses, walking stick and copy of the *Gita*. The Darshan Samiti has more fascinating displays, such as rare photographs, report cards from his schooldays, and even a collection of commemorative stamps from different countries!

- **National Gandhi Museum, Rajghat, New Delhi**

The National Gandhi Museum in New Delhi has an incredible collection of photographs and audio-visual material. These include recordings of speeches given by Gandhi and other leaders of the freedom movement, and 174 hours' worth of films about Gandhi! The museum has several unique galleries, such as the Spinning Wheel Gallery, which displays models of spinning wheels and looms and charts their evolution. The Martyrdom Gallery focuses on Gandhiji's assassination and even displays one of the bullets used.

- **Kirti Mandir and Museum, Porbandar, Gujarat**

Porbandar is Gandhiji's birthplace, and the Kirti Mandir located here is very special – it is the ancestral house where Gandhi was born. The house now displays paintings of Gandhi and his family, and you can even see the exact spot where Gandhi was born. A museum has been set up in the building next door, with a library and a collection of rare photographs.

- **Sabarmati Museum and Ashram, Ahmedabad**

In 1915, Gandhi started an Ashram in Kochrab, Ahmedabad, upon his return from South Africa. In 1917, the Ashram was relocated to the banks of the Sabarmati. Originally known as the Satyagraha Ashram, it remained Gandhi's home till 1930 and was thus an integral part of our nation's history. Most significantly, it was the site from which Gandhi's historic Dandi March began.

Today, the Ashram complex includes several sites of interest, including the Hriday Kunj, where Gandhiji stayed, and a guest house that hosted several important figures, including Nehru and Tagore. The museum displays exhibits relating to Gandhi's life and his contributions to the freedom struggle.

One unique feature of this museum is a portrait of Gandhi by Rajkishore Kapoor, which has been created out of groundnut and peanut shells!

- **Dandi Kutir, Gandhinagar, Ahmedabad**

The Dandi Kutir Museum is a unique museum, constructed in the shape of a heap of salt – a symbolic reminder of the way Gandhi used the idea of salt to unite the people and drive them to fight for independence. Unlike the other museums on this list, the Dandi Kutir doesn't have traditional displays of photographs and portraits. Instead, a range of immersive audio-visual materials depict Gandhi's early life, his days in London and South Africa, and his actions and contributions towards the freedom movement.

- **Gandhi Memorial Museum, Barrackpore, West Bengal**

The Gandhi Memorial Museum in Barrackpore aims to pay tribute to the Father of the Nation, with a special focus on his connections to the eastern parts of India. In addition to photographs, letters and personal effects, the museum also displays a life-size portrait of the Mahatma. The Bengal Gallery and Naokhali and Orissa Gallery focus on his visits to these regions of the country.

- **Gandhi Samarak Sangralaya, Patna**

This museum at Patna is well-known for the huge statue of Gandhi that stands within its complex. Like other museums dedicated to the Mahatma, it has a collection of pictures and photographs, as well as a library with books, magazines and audio-visual material related to Gandhi's life. The museum is free and open to all, and regularly holds film screenings and talks related to Gandhian values.

- **Gandhi National Memorial Society, Pune**

This museum is located in a site of historic significance, the Aga Khan Palace, where Gandhi and his wife Kasturba were imprisoned during the Quit India movement between August 1942 and May 1944. Kasturba passed away during this period and the museum includes a special memorial to her. Visitors to the museum can also see some of the rooms used by Gandhi and his wife during their imprisonment, as well as a picture gallery and collection of Gandhi's clothes and personal possessions. Interestingly, the famous film *Gandhi* was shot here!

- **Manibhavan Gandhi Sangralaya, Mumbai**

Gandhi spent 17 years living in Mani Bhavan and evolved several of his key ideas of non-violence and satyagraha here. Now a heritage building, the Mani Bhavan consists of a museum and an expansive library. On the second floor, you can even see the room where Gandhi lived and worked – the space from which he changed the nation's history!

- **Gandhi Teerth, Jalgaon, Maharashtra**

The Gandhi Teerth in Maharashtra is home to the Gandhi Research Foundation as well as a museum and library. The Khoj Gandhiji Ki Museum has a collection of audio-visual materials about Gandhi's life, highlighting the relevance of his message in today's world. The Gandhi Research Foundation has launched a movement to commemorate Mahatma Gandhi's 150th birth anniversary, focusing on spreading his ideals to the rural youth through workshops and other programmes. As part of this initiative, they even have solar-powered charkhas to spin khadi cloth!

- **Gandhi Memorial Museum, Madurai**

The Gandhi Memorial Museum of Madurai is located in the historic Tamukkam Palace. The location of the museum is important because it is here in Madurai that in 1921, Gandhi adopted his trademark dhoti. The museum displays a collection of photographs, paintings, and letters, as well as a special exhibition of handicrafts from the southern regions of Tamil Nadu, Mysore, Kerala and Andhra Pradesh.

> ### Beyond This List...
> The museums and memorials listed here aren't the only places where you can see representations of Gandhi. There are reminders of Gandhi almost everywhere you look, from the money in your wallet to the name of a street in your neighbourhood. You can do some research to find out places of interest around you that pay tribute to Gandhi or are a part of his history. Are there places you've passed by without realizing their significance? You might be inspired to plan a visit!

On This Day...

While Gandhi was making history, what else was happening around the world? You might be surprised to learn about some of these parallel events in history!

- Gandhi was born in 1869, the same year that Leo Tolstoy, whose writings greatly influenced Gandhi's ideals, published *War and Peace* as a complete book in Russia.

- Gandhi left Porbandar for Bombay in 1888, the year that the National Geographic Society was formed – a society that still exists, over a hundred years later, and which you might recognize from their iconic magazine or TV channel.

- In 1893, the year Gandhi moved to South Africa, the first movie studio was constructed in the United States. It was owned by someone whose name you might find familiar ... Thomas Edison!

- In 1909, Gandhi wrote *Hind Swaraj*, calling for Indian "home rule". A more trivial piece of history occurred this year, when a pig was carried on board an airplane for the first time, thus finally fulfilling the phrase "when pigs fly"!

- In April 1917, the famous Champaran Satyagraha began. The same month, the United States formally entered the First World War.

- In 1921, Gandhi famously announced the change in his attire, and would now stick to his trademark dhoti and shawl. This was also the year that Albert Einstein, who cites Gandhi as an inspiration, won the Nobel Prize in Physics.

- In January 1930, Gandhi and other leaders of India's freedom struggle declared "Purna Swaraj". This month also saw one of the biggest "supermoons" in history, when the moon was within 356,000 kilometres of the earth. This won't happen again until January 2257!

- On March 12, 1930, Gandhi began his iconic Dandi March to protest against the salt tax. Just one day later, on March 13, it was announced that a new planet had been discovered – Pluto!

- The Quit India Movement was launched in August 1942. It was a busy month for world events: the Disney film *Bambi* was released, and on a more serious note, Jews were being rounded up in various parts of Nazi-occupied Europe.

THE STORY OF MY LIFE

- Gandhi died in 1948. Famous people born in this year include novelist George R. R. Martin, politician Al Gore, actress Hema Malini and Charles, Prince of Wales!

> ### Time Travel: October 2nd Through the Years!
>
> It can be fascinating to pick one day in history and study it, across time and space. For example, you could look up events that have happened around the world on October 2nd. You could focus on a particular time period (such as the last ten years), or look at one year per decade – 2010, 2000, 1990, 1980 and so on. What's the most surprising or exciting fact you could find?

EXPLORING GANDHI IN TODAY'S WORLD

Gandhi and the World

There are commemorative sites in other parts of the world where Gandhi spent significant portions of his life, such as London and South Africa. Here are a few sites of interest:

- **Tolstoy Farm** – The Tolstoy Farm in South Africa, which is mentioned in the autobiography, was the site where Gandhi put into practice many of his ideals about living as a community. The site, located about 35 kilometres from Johannesburg, can still be visited today, and while much of the area is in disrepair, the original structure of Gandhi's house still stands. There are plans to restore this site and revive its function as a place to benefit local communities.

- **The Blue Plaques of London** – The iconic Blue Plaques of London, displayed on buildings around the city, mark sites of historic significance, where famous figures lived or worked. Two of these plaques mark locations where

Gandhi lived in London: a house on Baron's Court Road, where Gandhi lived when he was studying law, and Kingsley Hall, where he stayed in 1931.

There are even statues and monuments in commemoration of Gandhi, located all around the world! Here are just a few:

- The Gandhi World Peace Memorial at the **Lake Shrine Temple in California, USA**, which includes a shrine that holds a portion of his ashes. Interestingly, the US is apparently home to the largest number of Gandhi memorials outside of India – and it is a country that he never visited!

- A statue in **Pietermaritzburg, South Africa**, the city where Gandhi was forced to leave the first-class compartment of the train – an incident he recounts in his autobiography.

> ### Gandhi Around the World
> Do you think Gandhi's influence extends to every country? Pick a country and see if you can find any links to Gandhi. You could check for places of interest, or do research on whether any famous figures from the nation have been inspired by his ideals.

Gandhi's Influence

Gandhi's impact and influence travelled far and wide. National leaders, thinkers, artists and famous figures from all over the world have often cited him as their inspiration.

- "I believe that **Gandhi's views were the most enlightened of all the political men in our time.** We should strive to do things in his spirit: not to use violence in fighting for our cause, but by non-participation in anything you believe is evil." – Albert Einstein

- "**If humanity is to progress, Gandhi is inescapable.** He lived, thought, and acted, inspired by the vision of humanity evolving toward a world of peace and harmony." – Dr. Martin Luther King, Jr.

- "I have the greatest admiration and respect for Mahatma Gandhi. **He was a great human being with a deep understanding of human nature.** He made every effort to encourage the full development of the positive aspects of the human potential and to reduce or restrain the negative. His life has inspired me ever since I was a small boy." – The Dalai Lama

- **"Gandhi's magnificent example of personal sacrifice** and dedication in the face of oppression was one of his many legacies to our country and to the world ... The values of tolerance, mutual respect and unity for which he stood and acted had a profound influence on our liberation movement, and on my own thinking." – Nelson Mandela

- "Throughout my life, including my work as a young man on behalf of the urban poor, I have always found inspiration in the life of Gandhiji and in **his simple and profound lesson to be the change we seek in the world.** ... And just as he summoned Indians to seek their destiny, he influenced champions of equality in my own country." – Barack Obama

Tributes to Gandhi

Gandhi's assassination led to a tremendous outpouring of grief and people from all over the world paid tribute to his legacy. Here are just a few of the reactions to his death:

- "Great men and eminent men have monuments in bronze and marble set up for them, **but this man of divine fire managed in his life-time to become enmeshed in millions and millions of hearts** … He lives in the hearts of millions and he will live for immemorial ages." – Jawaharlal Nehru

- "**Far greater than all the warriors** who led the armies to battle was this little man, the bravest, the most tried friend of all." – Sarojini Naidu

- "Gandhiji's death is truly a loss to mankind … **India, indeed the world, will not see the like of him again**, perhaps, for centuries." – Lord Mountbatten

- **"Everyone concerned in the better future of mankind** must be deeply moved by the tragic death of Mahatma Gandhi … he has led a great nation on to its liberation." – Albert Einstein

- "There is no doubt Gandhi had great spiritual qualities and the one only hope, even though he is not with his people, is **that his influence had much of value to give to the rest of the world** and one hopes the very violence of his death will turn people away from violence." – Eleanor Roosevelt

Gandhi's Legacy

It's not just powerful political figures who have been inspired by Gandhi. Over the years, we can see his ideals of non-violence and passive resistance echoed in the actions of ordinary people ... with extraordinary results. Young people all over the world are leading powerful movements against injustice, and their methods may look familiar to you!

1. **Malala Yousafzai** has become well-known as a teenage activist, as she began to speak up after being attacked by the Taliban on her way to school. She continues to speak for women's and girls' right to education. She was co-winner of the Nobel Peace Prize in 2014, making her the youngest ever Nobel Laureate. Malala has said that her ideas of non-violence are inspired by leaders like Gandhi. At a speech to the UN Youth Assembly, she said, "I do not even hate the Talib who shot me. Even if there is a gun in my hands and he stands in front of me, I would not shoot

him. This is the philosophy of non-violence that I have learnt from Gandhiji, Badshah Khan and Mother Teresa".

> **"Let us pick up our books and our pens. They are our most powerful weapons. One teacher, one book, one pen, can change the world."**

2. **Greta Thunberg** is a teenager from Sweden who has entered the public eye for her work on climate change. In August 2008, she began a one-person strike outside the Swedish parliament, calling for more attention to the threat of global warming. Her strike, and the sign she held, which said "School Strike for Climate", began to encourage schoolchildren across the country, and later the world, to do the same. By 2019, millions of students began to participate in coordinated climate strikes around the world. Greta's strategy of non-violent protest and community involvement, and her focus on the importance of taking care of the environment, all echo Gandhi's ideals.

> **"Change is coming, whether you like it or not."**

3. **Melati and Isabel Wijsen** are two teenagers from Bali, who were inspired to make a difference after sitting through a lesson about inspiring figures including Nelson Mandela and Gandhi. They started a movement, Bye Bye Plastic Bags, in 2013, to promote eco-friendly practices among the children in their local communities. BBPB now exists around the world! This worldwide movement began in a

familiar way – with a hunger strike. Melati says that this was directly inspired by Gandhi. "He also had peaceful ways of reaching his goals, of getting attention, so that was a huge inspiration for us," she says.

> **"You see, we didn't want to wait until we were older to start making a difference."**

Gandhi in Your Life

You can do your own research to find other activists, leaders, and people around you whose actions and beliefs can be linked to Gandhi's ideals. You might even be inspired to take some small steps of your own!

What Can You Do? Slow Fashion

"The world has enough for everyone's needs, but not everyone's greed." – Mahatma Gandhi

Slow Fashion is an approach to fashion, which considers the processes and resources required to make clothing, particularly focusing on sustainability. It involves buying better-quality garments that will last for longer and values fair treatment of people, animals and the environment.

The term Slow Fashion was coined by Kate Fletcher of the Centre for Sustainable Fashion.

In 2018, 150 billion garments were made, but 50 billion garments were never sold, and another 50 billion were sold at discount.

With major global clothing brands having to burn tonnes of unsold garments every year in spite of ongoing sustainability efforts to close the loop in fashion, slow fashion seems to be the need of the hour. It has three underlying principles:

- Made from high quality, sustainable material

- Developed in local stores rather than huge chain enterprises

- Locally sourced, produced and sold garments

In Gandhi's own words, "Not mass production, but production by the masses." Ahimsa is at the heart of the Slow Fashion Movement, which focuses on quality, where each village would thrive in their own eco-system of skills, services, production and distribution. Gandhi wanted to give them the status of "village republics".

He also believed in the idea of aparigraha, which means non-possession and urges one not to hoard anything that we do not need today. One of Gandhi's philosophies is, "The less you possess, the less you want, the better you are."

Gandhi believed that we are mere "trustees" or custodians of our environment and owe it to ourselves to pass it on to the next generation in a good condition.

Small Steps

You could try to practice slow fashion in your day-to-day life. This could mean that you buy less clothes through the year or buy from local shops instead of big brands.

You could jot down more ideas on how to join Gandhi's movement of aparigraha and ahimsa by practicing slow fashion in your everyday life.

More books on Gandhi from HarperCollins

Being Gandhi by Paro Anand

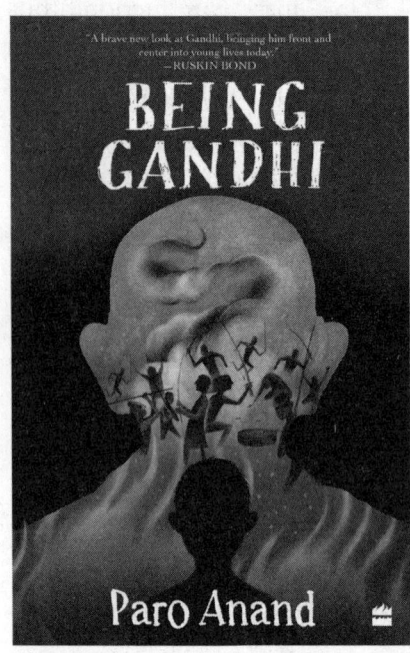

How many times are kids supposed to study Gandhi? Come September and out comes the bald head wig, round glasses, white dhoti, tall stick … that's about the extent of how today's kids engage with the Mahatma.

Chandrashekhar is one such teen. Bored by the annual Gandhi projects, he wonders if his teacher is being too unreasonable in asking them to "BE" Gandhi. And then, his world is shaken by events that rock him to the core, forcing him to dig deep and not just find his 'inner Gandhi', but become Gandhi. Not for a day or two. But, maybe even, for life.

This is a novel that explores, not Gandhi the man or his life as a leader, but really the Gandhian way that must remain relevant to us. Especially today when the world is becoming increasingly steeped in violence and hate.

Tales of Young Gandhi by Janhavi Prasada

Encouraged by his co-workers, Mohandas Karamchand Gandhi decided to write his autobiography in the 1920s.

The Story of My Experiments with Truth went on to inspire generations of people worldwide. As on millions of others, the memoir of an ordinary man who achieved extraordinary feats had a strong impact on Janhavi Prasada when she first read it. And with that was born her desire to share his path of peace, and the inspiration she had found in his work, with as many people as she could. As she realized, he was much ahead of his times not only as a thinker but also as a doer.

Exquisitely illustrated, with visual content that Janhavi collected over eight years of travel to Porbandar, London and South Africa, *Tales of Young Gandhi* retells the story of a fascinating life and hopes to introduce a new generation of readers to the Mahatma.